CHINA: 1

CHINA: Behind the Mask

By *Warren H. Phillips*
and *Robert Keatley*

DOW JONES BOOKS
PRINCETON, NEW JERSEY

Introduction

We know so little about China. For a generation it has been a land apart—a name, a place, a presence but nearly as remote in mind and space as the planet Jupiter.

Part of China's isolation was its own choice; part was by diplomatic design. The result was the same: a prolonged interruption in the normal flow of goods, people, and information. China barred most Westerners, scholars and reporters as well as diplomats. It spoke to the world through its propaganda organs in Peking, and told only what it chose to tell. Apart from that, the world saw the real China and heard the real China only through the keyhole that was Hong Kong. The information was fragmentary, episodic, and often misleading. China succeeded in closing the world out.

Yet China's presence on the world stage grew. It could not be otherwise. With its 800 million people, its militant brand of Communist ideology, its political and military power, China was a country impossible to ignore. We had long viewed China as bellicose and belligerent in its foreign affairs—a danger to its neighbors. China, for its part, viewed itself as the endangered one. The threat was seen in Peking to come from the Soviet Union at least as much as from the Western powers.

In 1971, for reasons of its own, China's government began to relax its posture toward the United States. For the first time in more than 20 years, it agreed to permit visits by selected American newsmen. More important, it permitted the newsmen—within certain limits—to report first-hand on the changes in China and its people.

Among the small number of professional newsmen permitted to get a fresh and close-up view of China today were three representing The Wall Street Journal: Warren H. Phillips, now president of Dow Jones & Company, which publishes the Journal; Robert Keatley, the Journal's diplomatic correspondent stationed in Washington, D.C.; and William Hartley, the Wall Street Journal correspondent based in Tokyo. The articles by Phillips and Keatley, published in 1971 and 1972 and gathered together here for the first time, provide a panoramic but sharply etched picture of China's economic, political, and social status. A gem of a report on a Chinese trade fair in late 1972 by Hartley is included here, as well as a transcript of the extraordinary interview that Premier Chou En-lai gave American editors in Peking on the downfall and death of Lin Piao, once the designated successor of Mao Tse-tung.

What sets these reports apart—and makes them interesting as well as important—is the sharp focus on people, rather than on things, the specific, rather than the generalization. Thus we see Chou En-lai, an intelligent and witty host, going through some intellectual and verbal gymnastics explaining the demise of Lin Piao. Through Phillips, we meet Wang Chi-mu, a girl of 17; Wang Chin-hua, a wheatfield worker in Yenan; and Yung Hai-ying, a student at Peking University—three young people whose lives are harbingers of tomorrow's China.

We meet Liu Shu-hsien, a farmer of 56 who looks 70 and is on the front line of China's constant fight to feed its growing population, and Yang Hsiao-ping, a woman on the Shensi Province family-planning committee who believes that "public opinion" is the most effective way of encouraging young people to marry later and have small families.

Keatley introduces us to Chiang Ting-hua, one of China's "responsible persons" in a Shenyang locomotive factory, and to Lo Kwei-shi, a soldier who is manager of a secondary school near Peking.

There are others, and through their words and actions—and the perceptiveness of the reporters—we get a better understanding of social and political vibrancy in China today. Conversations, formal and casual, also suggest the depth of misinformation and dogma the Chinese have about the outside world.

Like The Wall Street Journal itself, which regularly uncovers intriguing stories in the most unlikely places, the Journal reporters in China found fascinating bits of information in fish markets as well as formal banquets, in school rooms, farmers' kitchens, and railroad cars. Out of the sights, sounds, and images gathered come articles that begin to fill the void in our knowledge of China—a vast land that holds about one-fourth of the world's entire population.

Keatley and Phillips describe what they saw, tell how the Chinese people live, explain what they perceive Peking's aspirations to be, and then evaluate how good the performance seems to date. They also raise some questions a visit or two leave unanswered, or which simply can't be answered—such as the impact of the inevitable leadership changes.

Recently, a Chinese diplomat at the United Nations complained mildly to Keatley about the press coverage his country now enjoys in the United States. It's too uncritical, he said, adding: "Everything in China is not good; we still have serious problems and there are many things wrong there."

Introduction

The authors agree. And they provide the necessary balance here.

A word about the authors: Bob Keatley first visited China in 1971 after having had nearly a dozen years of reporting for the Journal, much of it from Asia. Accompanying him to China was his wife, Anne, who is knowledgeable in the Peking dialect as well as a capable photographer. Keatley returned to Peking in 1972 as part of the American press group accompanying President Nixon.

Warren Phillips worked as Journal correspondent in Europe in the late 1940s and early 1950s before returning to the United States and eventually becoming Managing Editor of the Journal in 1957, a post he held for more than eight years before moving up the corporate ladder. In the four-week tour of China with 21 other American editors in September and October of 1972, Phillips travelled more than 4,000 miles in China, wrote 10 articles, and took many of the photographs that appear in this book.

Phillips notes that the Chinese plainly mobilized to give the American editors the best possible presentation of their system. But more often than not, he says, "The Chinese were candid in answering our skeptical questions. They made no effort to prevent us from talking to students, workers, farmers, and housewives whom we selected at random, or from knocking on doors and visiting homes at random. We saw much of the bad side—the poverty, the pervasive totalitarianism —as well as the good."

In essence, then, this is a collection of discerning and important articles, written with wit and flair, about China today—China behind the mask.

Contents

Appendix

The Quiet People

THE visitor awakens on his first morning in the Peking Hotel to what sounds strangely like the din of New York traffic.

Car horns are honking insistently. And they keep it up throughout the nine days spent in the capital. Yet there is no traffic. Or at least there's none worthy of the name.

Outside on the broad expanse of Chang An Avenue, the city's main thoroughfare, and on the side streets leading into it, there are a few buses, a few trucks and only a handful of official government cars. There are fewer motor vehicles on the streets than in New York or Chicago at four in the morning.

Yet all Peking drivers lean hard on their horns to warn away the swarms of bicyclists who otherwise would take over the streets on their way to and from work and on other errands.

It's the same in Canton, Shanghai and other Chinese cities—the impatient sounds of the auto age. Yet this is a country with no private cars except those owned by foreigners, a country where you can travel for over three weeks and spot only two filling stations. It's a country with only slightly over 1,000 miles of paved highways besides the gravel and dirt ones; they serve a nation larger than the U.S. and inhabited by almost four times as many people. It's also a country where it's common to see men and sometimes even women with ropes over their shoulders pulling carts that are laden with concrete utility poles or sacks of farm produce or that are piled high with bricks, bales of cotton or lumber.

What goes on in the minds of those men and women on the bicycles or pulling the carts like beasts of burden or riding in the trucks or official cars? China's people, like the country itself, are a kaleidoscope of contrasts and contradictions.

Screen out the horns and the tinkle of bicycle bells, for example, and there is a puzzling quiet about this capital of the People's Republic of China. Seven million of China's 800 million people live here. As they cycle purposefully along or stroll with their children in the parks, they rarely shout to one another or burst out in laughter or loud conversation.

Many other visitors also have remarked on the striking contrast with the Chinese communities in Hong Kong or New York's Chinatown or with the China that some diplomats recall from before World War II. Many theories are offered to explain the relative quiet that surrounds the world's greatest mass of humanity.

"They're more subdued because they're more controlled, more disciplined," one diplomat says. "The old fire in China has been put under a hood."

Another contends: "People are good to each other, they're taught in the schools they must help each other and get along with each other to live successfully in such crowded conditions. They're inculcated from the word 'go' in compatibility, toning down, discipline, the ability to live together in greater harmony."

"Hong Kong is full of shouting peddlers," says Chi Chan, a member of the staff of China Reconstructs, a monthly magazine. "We don't have that here anymore. Maybe that's why it seems quieter. Also, people now are serious about their work, about everything they do."

"The old Chinese humor has disappeared in the face of the grandeur of the task they have undertaken, and it has yielded to a severe austerity and an incredible degree of morality," says Odile Cail, who spent years here with her French diplomat husband. Her comment appears in the new Fodor's "Peking" she recently wrote.

Penetrating the reality of China, in this as in other areas, is difficult for any Westerner. He can only observe that the Chinese seem calm and self-assured with a sense of pride. They're often animated when talking of their work. Could it be that they suppress spontaneity in regard to themselves lest it be construed as expressing individuality when the emphasis is on order, discipline and the collective society? Like the wearing of the same somber blue or gray tunics and trousers, it may be an effort to sink into anonymity and not stand out. After all, individuality is a quality hardly in vogue in China these days.

Spontaneity and human warmth aren't very far beneath the surface, though. Young men and women walk along the roadsides collecting colorful fall leaves on their days off; others can be seen near the Great Wall north of Peking collecting bouquets of wild yellow flowers with their children. A greeting from a strange foreigner or a request to photograph a family's child usually brings instant, broad smiles to faces that were impassive a moment before.

Lapses of discipline are the rule when it comes to pushing and shoving to squeeze aboard a packed bus; a Peking crowd is the match of any crush of New York commuters.

Tears well in the eyes of a visitor's Chinese friend of only a week or two as the moment for parting arrives. And there is nothing restrained in the enthusiasm of the greeting extended to passing visitors by children and adults alike in many places away from Shanghai and Peking as they rush to the roadsides to wave and clap and as their faces burst into warm smiles of welcome.

Egalitarianism now is the order of the day, and it is fairly widely and seriously practiced. Kuan Pao-ling, chairman of the revolutionary committee that manages Textile Factory No. 4 in Sian, about 420 miles southwest of Peking, lives with the three other members of his family in a one-and-a-half-room apartment just like those occupied by his workers. The apartment is in a building where workers in his factory live, and he pays the same rent and electricity charge.

He doesn't have the use of a car for personal errands. And about 80 skilled technical workers in the 6,400-man factory earn higher salaries than he does. This is general throughout the country and is in contrast to the privileged managerial class in Russia.

Yet sometimes there are lapses in the egalitarianism. A visiting group of American editors were among the foreign guests one evening at a banquet in the Great Hall of the People at which Premier Chou En-lai, Vice Premier Li Hsien-nien, Mao Tse-tung's wife, Chiang Ching, and numerous other dignitaries marked the 23rd anniversary of their government.

In contrast with similar functions in the U.S. and elsewhere, the head table wasn't raised above the level of the other guests by means of a dais. Austere and somber Mao-style tunics were the fashion with most of the civilians; the generals wore their uniforms without insignia of rank to distinguish them from the privates, as has been the custom here since the mid-1960s.

But there was nothing egalitarian about the 11 dishes served. They ranged from Peking duck and balls of lobster meat to that local delicacy, sea slugs. And there was nothing egalitarian about the long lines of limousines that carried the officials and guests away.

Nor was there anything egalitarian about the distance at which the crowds of onlookers were kept from the Great Hall. Or perhaps it should be said that the discipline of the crowd itself is what kept it at a distance. Unarmed army men in baggy green uniforms stood about 25 yards apart in front of the crowd but needed to make no effort to hold it back. There was no pushing or surging forward. The wall of people just stood in place, silent and obedient.

To say the people are regimented isn't to say the enormous majority necessarily are unhappy. However, it's certain that many are, in a society where you can't choose your career or job or where you will live, or travel to another part of the country without permission, or speak your mind freely without fear of the consequences. Between 1,000 and 2,000 flee to Hong Kong each month out of frustration, and there must be many times this number without means to get close enough to the border to make the attempt. The regimentation must be most stifling to the intellectuals.

But the vast sea of humanity that tills the soil and works the looms and the steel furnaces never had exposure to a free life under a democracy. For this mass, it has been a long history of rule by an elite of scholar-officials, or mandarins. The strict hierarchical system of Confucianism was carried right down into the village, the clan and the family.

A high value has always been placed on conformity and social approval. "When the Chinese act opportunistically (as all conformists must do from time to time), they are engaged in culturally approved behavior," according to Francis L. K. Hsu, an anthropologist and China scholar at Northwestern University. "Their problem has always been how to make the individual live according to the accepted customs and rules of conduct, not how to enable him to rise above them."

The Chinese have a popular adage: "The tall tree is crushed by the wind first."

Dennis Bloodworth, a London Observer correspondent, in his book, "The Chinese Looking Glass," puts the same thought another way: "The Westerner is forever trying to alter the world to suit himself while the Chinese alters himself to suit the world."

The Chinese masses, more than 80% of whom live on the land, measure their present circumstances by what they knew before, certainly not by an American experience so alien to them. And at least destitution and epidemic disease aren't facing them as they have through China's history.

One wag has commented that they have graduated from destitution to poverty. In some respects this is true. Housing often is poor and overcrowded, a true consumer-goods economy unknown and life still Spartan in the extreme by American standards. But the neighborhood stores in the parts of the country we visited are amply stocked with fruit, vegetables, meat, fish, pastries and other food. Clothing, though austere with little selection, nevertheless is clean, neat and adequate.

No one can peer behind the well-scrubbed, healthy-looking faces and see inside the minds of 800 million Chinese. But they give the impression of measuring their material well-being relative to their own standards and concluding they are better off than they were. The vast majority seem almost relaxed in their regimentation, as if they had concluded that the terrible price for their improved material well-being wasn't too high.

As long as this is so, chances are they'll choose not to rock the boat.

Two incidents illustrate the human and the totalitarian sides of Chinese life.

From a sixth-floor window of the Peking Hotel—the same window through which the din of auto horns comes—a visitor can glimpse some of the contrasts in how today's China lives. In the distance are the high walls behind which the Ming and Manchu emperors lived, the orange-tiled roofs of the Forbidden City's ancient palaces, Tien An Men Square and the Great Hall of the People, massed red flags flying from its roof to mark a state occasion. There is all the panoply of authoritarian power, both past and present.

In the foreground beneath the hotel window are tightly packed one-story houses. One courtyard nearby is used by several families living in what might once have been a single L-shaped house. It now is divided into several apartments, whose back doors open into the court.

A mother brushes and braids a little girl's hair. A man sweeps the courtyard clean after a breakfast cooked outdoors on a primitive charcoal stove. Three little boys prance around the courtyard, waving their arms. A younger one follows them at a gallop. The mother, her work on her daughter's hair completed, begins to wash her own in a bowl on the floor of the yard.

All seem in high spirits. None are aware they are being observed. Here, in the shadow of the seats of power, the universality of family life goes on, much as it does in a hundred other lands.

Tempted to know more about this particular family, I knock on the door a few days later and ask, through an interpreter, if an overseas traveler might visit for a short while.

Inside is the Chang family. The mother, Wang Hsu-chen, is a pretty, animated woman of 31 who works in a hospital admissions office. Her husband, Chang Nai-hua, 33, is a construction worker. They, their two children, her sister's three children, her mother and her father live packed into two small rooms. The sister and brother-in-law live in a single room in another house nearby.

Outside in the courtyard is the stove on which the family does its cooking. A homemade wooden canopy protects it from rain. The stove is brought into one of the bedrooms in winter to provide heat. Water comes from a tap in the courtyard.

It's hard to visualize four adults and five children squeezing into the two double beds and two singles that occupy most of the space in the two rooms. Or how eating, schoolwork and general family life can be conducted in such sardine-can quarters.

But Wang Hsu-chen isn't complaining. Because her mother cares for her children and her sister's during the day, she, her husband, her sister, her sister's husband and her father all are able to work. She makes 38 yuan a month ($16.53, at 43.5 cents per yuan) and her husband 60 yuan; but among the five working members of the family, they earn 280 yuan ($121.80) a month. That may not sound like much in U.S. dollar terms, but the prices are lower here.

Rent for her two rooms and her sister's room takes eight yuan a month, and food requires 200 yuan for the two households. The rest goes for clothing and incidentals, with something left over for savings—20 yuan some months, as much as 50 other times.

"With five of us earning money, we have enough to keep our life at a very good level," Wang Hsu-chen says. "It's been improving gradually. My husband and I each got a raise of 10 yuan last August, and the prices of food and the things we buy for everyday use have been stable —sometimes even declining, like meat. And where we work, there are medical services that are free for workers. We have everything we want—a radio, a sewing machine, watches for everyone."

For the present, they measure their lives against

what they've known in the past and what others around them have, and they feel prosperous. Or so they say. There is no reason, in watching their eyes and the enthusiasm with which they speak, to doubt their sincerity.

"Before Liberation, workers like us couldn't earn enough to support their families, to feed their children," Wang Hsu-chen says. "Now we have nothing to worry about, even if someone gets sick. I'm happy our children were born in the new China."

This sentiment obviously is widely shared, but it's just as obvious it isn't unanimous. Many of those who have devoted their lives to cultivation of the mind, and particularly those who have known Western life, must find the blanket of enforced conformity that lies over China most suffocating.

It's a sobering experience to sit at a table at Peking University and talk with Professor Chou Yi-liang of the history department, who studied at Harvard from 1939 to 1946 and earned his Ph.D. there; Prof. Wu Chu-chen of the English department, who is a graduate of Columbia University; and Prof. Chou Pei-yuan, who studied physics at the University of Chicago and Cal Tech between 1924 and 1928.

Chou Pei-yuan was vice president of the university before the Cultural Revolution. Now he is vice chairman of the revolutionary committee that runs the school. The chairman, who wasn't present, is Wang Lien-lung, an army officer. He replaced Prof. Chou's former boss, university president Lu Ping, who the professor says is "participating in physical labor" for following "revisionist" policies.

Chou Pei-yuan begins nervously to tell us about the university, but the conversation soon is taken over and dominated by a crisp, self-assured Communist Party administrator named Li Chia-kuan, who wears his hair cropped close to his skull. Mr. Li wasn't an educator but was helping to supervise factories in the Peking area before he was sent to the university with seven military men and six workers in 1968 as a member of a Mao Tse-tung Thought Propaganda Team. It is quickly obvious who wields the authority.

English Prof. Wu tells of being sent to work on a farm in Kiangsi Province for two years, along with other faculty members, to rid himself of any superiority he might feel toward manual laborers. "They were two of the happiest years of my life," he contends. In 1971, he joined his students for a three-month stint shoveling coal in a mine.

"All of us elderly professors, whether Western-educated or not, had undergone bourgeois educations," chimes in historian Chou Yi-liang, the Harvard man. "We not only had bourgeois educations but a lot of feudal thinking. All of us needed reeducation. Liu Shao-chi (the former chief of state, who was purged during the Cultural Revolution) gave us very high salaries and comfortable material surroundings and had us carry on bourgeois education. We didn't know what really was meant by bourgeois education. Only in the Cultural Revolution did we go among the peasants and workers and were we reeducated."

Are these words the required litany of a soul in torment? Or does he believe what he is saying, his mind conditioned in Pavlovian fashion by unimaginable pressures? Either way, the visitor finds it a searing encounter.

The Image Makers

REPORTING from China produces mixed feelings: Some of the frustrations of negotiating an obstacle course, pleasant surprise at hosts more helpful than anticipated, and gratitude that we don't have to cope with the problems of Chinese journalists.

With other members of a delegation from the American Society of Newspaper Editors, we visit the Peking Arts and Crafts Factory on our first day in the capital. Some 1,260 workers are carving jade and ivory, making settings for rings and brooches, painting scenes on the shells of eggs and doing other art work.

We stop to talk to some of them at random. One is Tien Yu-ling, 31, a design technician.

"What's the most important thing Mao Tse-tung has done for your life?" he is asked.

"Now I have become the true master of the country," says Mr. Tien. "He taught me to know I am serving the people. Also, we have the right to give our opinion in state affairs."

"How do you know your opinion counts?"

"The leader of the Party here collects the opinions of the workers," he replies. "The Party will consider the opinion of the masses when making policy."

"What do you think about Lin Piao (who was Mao's chosen successor before being accused of plotting to seize power)?"

"He died. I think he was a traitor."

"How did you learn that?"

"I was told by my superior authorities."

While this exchange is taking place, a young woman stands in the background, busily taking notes. She does this each time we stop to talk to members of the work force.

We question her, and she says her name is An Pao-tung and she is on the staff of the 13-member revolutionary committee that runs the plant. We ask why she is taking notes. "We want to know what your criticisms are so we can improve our work," she says.

Later, we determine from the revolutionary committee's lady chairman, Wei Shu-ling, that about 10 groups of foreign visitors a week are taken through this factory. We ask whether the workers are trained how to receive foreign visitors.

"Every week the workers have study periods," says Mrs. Wei. "They study the works of Chairman Mao, current events and technical matters. There are no particular studies of how to welcome visitors. There may be brought up in these discussions some questions of what foreign visitors may be interested in."

Miss An's notes form the basis for discussing questions foreign visitors might ask. One assumes this can only lead to discussion of how best to respond.

"It helps us to improve our presentation," says one of the guides.

It is clear we are visiting a showplace factory and the responses by the workers to our questions, though possibly sincere, are not necessarily spontaneous.

Similar "presentations" mark our visits to a number of other factories, communes and schools. But our 24 days inside China are much less restricted to stage-managed segments than we had anticipated.

Our delegation of 22 is accompanied by 13 Chinese interpreters, guides and men to handle the logistics arrangements. They come from Chinese news organizations and the Foreign Ministry. As we expected, they don't take us into every corner of China that we suggest visiting. But neither do they act as if their job is to try to isolate us and shield us from the distasteful sides of Chinese life.

We wander into residential neighborhoods of our selection, knocking at random on doors of houses that are a far cry from the model, modern blocks of apartments. We then go inside to look at the residents' accommodations and ask them about their lives. We walk the aisles of cross-country trains, stopping to talk with riders we select in the coaches. We question people at random on the streets of the cities, and in farm villages, again knocking on doors we pick out.

Members of our group who have visited Russia say there is no comparison. Our reporting in China is far less restricted. When a group of American editors, accustomed to asking blunt questions and intolerant of evasion, can toast our Chinese hosts for their helpfulness without a trace of hypocrisy, the toast is deserved.

They work long and hard to fulfill our requests. They mobilize to see that we get the best possible view of their system and what they are doing in China today. They naturally would prefer to present a favorable view if possible. Their purpose, with us and other foreign visitors, obviously is to have us convey to the world the image of a relaxed and stable China. China hopes to win with smiles and the appearance of reasonableness the influence in the world it failed in the past to win with bluster.

But whether the view we get is favorable or otherwise, most of the Chinese we deal with, although certainly not all, don't duck the tough questions and seem willing to give us a view of their country that is more candid than we anticipated. Perhaps this reflects their sophistication, next to the Russians, in pursuing their goals. Perhaps it also reflects a confidence in their achievements and the relative satisfaction of the population at this moment in time.

It's true, of course, that we require the services of an interpreter. And even if he were not present, it's questionable whether people would expose their souls to any stranger, much less a foreigner. Many of our impressions come by use of our eyes, and also by indirection.

It's interesting, though, that foreigners of Chinese extraction, including Chinese-Americans, are being allowed to visit here in increasing numbers. The Chinese are confident enough to let these visitors, who know the language, roam relatively freely and mix with Chinese relatives and friends who might not be so inhibited about revealing their feelings.

At Peking University one afternoon and evening, administrators and faculty members answer a fusillade of probing, embarrassing questions. They don't seek escape by replying "no comment" to some, or bringing the interview to a close. The questioning goes on for six hours. We all miss dinner.

That same evening, I select six students and go into a dormitory room to talk about China and America. They are students of English and no translator or official is present.

One question they're asked is whether it doesn't strike them as strange that today's party line so often is tomorrow's heresy, today's hero tomorrow's villain. Liu Shao-chi was chief of state and Mao's right-hand man —and then was denounced and ousted as a "capitalist roader." Next Lin Piao was picked by Mao to be his successor—until he was accused of being a traitor. The U.S. was castigated for years as an imperialistic, warmongering nation—and now President Nixon and even representatives of The Wall Street Journal are welcomed here.

"The American people are great and always have been great," one of the students responds. As for those other fellows, "they originally were traitors, sham Marxists who sought high rank in order to deceive the people."

The official explanation is that every step forward and every victory angers the "bourgeoisie and its agents within the Party" and is therefore bound to encounter resistance from them. As they come out into the open one after another, the workers and peasants must ceaselessly sweep them away, it's contended.

A puzzled look comes over the students' faces. "Does this strike you as strange?" one of them asks.

For both Americans and Chinese, a newsman's life here has its ups and downs, its moments in the spotlight and its moments in the shadows.

The American editors dine with Chinese editors one evening at the Peking Duck Restaurant. Emerging afterward, they find a large crowd gathered across the street from the restaurant and on either side of it. The crowd has been waiting in the chill night air, perhaps for an hour or more, to catch a glimpse of the odd-looking foreigners.

People here are not yet as accustomed to seeing foreigners as we had assumed. Everywhere we go crowds gather and adults and children stare directly and unblinkingly at the Americans with their strange faces and even stranger clothes. On one occasion, a woman bicyclist stares so intently she fails to watch where she's going and falls off her bike.

"I feel like an astronaut," says one of the editors.

Our host for the evening at the Peking Duck is Chu Mu-chih, director of Hsinhua, China's state news agency. He, too, has had his moments in the spotlight as his moments in the shadows. He has put in several stints at a May 7 school in Shansi Province—a school where political education is advanced by planting and harvesting rice and hauling manure alongside the peasants until an official is able to empathize with them.

Hsinhua's news staff goes to the country for such "reintegration with the masses" for six months at a time, on a rotating basis. Some 110 are there now. Over 200 members of the staff of The People's Daily, the Communist Party newspaper, also are at such camps now—as are professional, managerial and Party workers from most other institutions in the country.

But Mr. Chu's absence from his job wasn't average. He was taken out of action at Hsinhua for more than two years. It seems he violated Chairman Mao's instruction that journalism should be used as a weapon to advance socialism. He had been guilty of reporting news as news.

But today, "remodeled," he is back in the boss' chair.

The American visitors receive rare invitations to visit the Hsinhua and People's Daily headquarters and talk with their top editors. The behind-the-scenes look at how China collects and disseminates news and propaganda to its 800 million people is professionally intriguing.

But the exposure to American newsmen must be an even more unusual experience for the Chinese. Never have they been confronted with such a barrage of direct questioning by foreigners about their personal problems in keeping ideologically pure, their professional operating methods and their government's inconsistencies.

"I don't mean to be offensive," begins Ed Murray of the Detroit Free Press during the visit to the Hsinhua news agency, "but do your correspondents abroad file background information—on military developments, say—in addition to news dispatches for publication?"

(Answer: "No.")

"How does The People's Daily confer and agree on its more important editorials?" another editor asks when we visit that paper.

(Answer: "To tell you frankly we are the organ of the Central Committee of the Communist Party in China. Leaders of our paper often participate in the important meetings of the committee. We should know the exact line of our Party. If we can't do our work independently our committee would have fired us.")

"What's your newspaper's Department for Mass Work?"

(Answer: "Letters to the Editor.")

"Were any of your people caught on the wrong side when past leaders such as Liu Shao-chi or Lin Piao were denounced?"

(Answer: "No.")

"What about Wu Leng-hsi (who had been chief editor of The People's Daily and also director of Hsinhua for several years)? Didn't he have a problem of this sort?" I ask.

(Answer: "That is not correct, Mr. Phillips. Mr. Wu is ill with heart disease and hypertension.")

Either our host at The People's Daily lacks some of the candor shown by others on our trip, or perhaps the passage of time has blurred his memory. In 1967 the Red Guards publicly accused Mr. Wu of being a "bourgeois reactionary" and in September 1968 he was branded a "counter-revolutionary revisionist" in the pages of his own People's Daily. He vanished, presumably to be "reeducated" and "remolded," as they say here, and only reappeared in August 1972.

He is indeed ill, but is already participating in the drafting of the most important People's Daily editorials and is slated to resume a leading role at the newspaper if his health permits. Like Mr. Chu of Hsinhua and many others who fell from grace during the Cultural Revolution, he has been rehabilitated.

A Foreign Ministry official, asked later whether the Chinese editors minded the grilling, replied: "No, it helps us understand each other. And if we are to be friends, we must understand each other."

It's also good practice if Chinese from many fields are going to start visiting the U.S. in increasing numbers, as they indicate they will. After all, they'll have to start coping with blunt questioners from the press the moment they step off the plane.

Three Young Lives

THIS is the story of three young people whose lives are harbingers of tomorrow's China.

Wang Chi-mu, a girl of 17, is a high-school student at Peking's Middle School No. 31.

Wang Chin-hua, 21, graduated from a Peking junior high school in 1970 and was sent to work in the wheat fields and cornfields around Yenan, in Shensi Province. He hopes to have an opportunity to go to college.

Yung Hai-ying, 23, is a member of the People's Liberation Army and is starting his third year at Peking University as a student of English.

The youth of any country hold that nation's future in its hands. This is no less true in China, whose plains and valleys contain one-fourth of mankind. Two-thirds of China's 800 million people are under age 30. Half the population is under 18, compared with 30% in the U.S. America's total population is only about half as large as the under-18 segment of China's sea of humanity.

How the minds of Wang Chi-mu, Wang Chin-hua and Yung Hai-ying develop as they proceed through China's fast-changing educational system and take their places in society will help shape answers to several important questions. They are questions of significance not only to China's future but also to that of the U.S. and other nations.

These are the questions:

As literacy increases and education expands, can young people be taught to think creatively and skeptically about engineering and agricultural problems without those habits of thought spilling over into other areas—such as politics?

Will China's new educational system be able to train the kind of educated adults the country will need most to develop its enormous potential?

And, perhaps most important, can the political indoctrination that permeates education in China make Chinese youths accept their leaders' calls for sacrifice, conformity and blind obedience if frustrations develop in their future lives? Members of this generation haven't known any system in their lifetimes other than Maoist communism and have been ceaselessly indoctrinated since nursery school. On the other hand, they lack the firsthand experience with the "bad old days" of hunger and hopeless poverty that makes today's China attractive to so many of their elders.

Secondhand tales of the U.S. depression don't impress American youth as much as the experience itself impressed their parents and grandparents. Will China's youths be different? Will they be satisfied if their own standards of living and job opportunities don't rise and provide them with a life of the sort they must occasionally daydream about?

The answers lie with the future. But a closer look at the lives of Wang Chi-mu, Wang Chin-hua and Yung Hai-ying provide some clues in trying to discern the shape of China's tomorrow.

We first pick out Chi-mu at random from a group of Middle School No. 31 students on the school playing field. She is a sweet-faced, smiling girl, dressed in gray trousers and the traditional blue tunic that is like a uniform in Chinese society today. Peeking from beneath it at the neck is a red-and-white-striped polo shirt.

Chi-mu and her classmates have just finished a session of marching and maneuvering almost identical to the close-order drill that U.S. servicemen receive in their basic military training. It was accompanied by stirring martial music played from a public-address-system loudspeaker near the playing field.

The military drill is part of her physical-education course. However, all students over 16, girls included, are members of the militia. The best of the older students get target-shooting practice on holidays.

Chi-mu was born in Sinkiang Province in the northwest and moved to Peking with her parents when she was four. She went to nursery school here and then to primary school, where she joined the Red Guards during the 1966-69 Cultural Revolution and helped "to criticize the revisionist line in education but not our teachers."

Middle School No. 31—which was the Chung Teh Missionary School, run by British missionaries, before the Communists came to power—was closed for most of 1966 and 1967, as were most other schools in China.

Four years ago Chi-mu's parents were transferred to northeast China, but she stayed behind with an aunt to continue her schooling here. Her father is a department head in a petrochemical plant, and her mother is a quality-control inspector at the same factory. Chi-mu sees her parents during her winter and summer vacations and during her parents' vacations.

Her year consists of eight months of classroom study, one month of working in an outside factory or a workshop attached to the school, one month working on a farm and two months of vacation.

Ma An-chum, vice chairman of the revolutionary

committee running the school and a former math teacher, explains that one of the fundamental changes made at this and all other schools since the Cultural Revolution has been the integration of theoretical knowledge with practical experience. In the U.S. it might be called "relevance."

The school opened four of its own workshops, called small factories, to give students industrial knowledge. Under the direction of Wan Tin-chen, 67, a retired worker, students in one workshop use lathes, a 25-mm. vertical drill and a shaver to make cable blocks, stainless-steel rings and other parts for a nearby factory, which supplies raw materials and also helped provide obsolete equipment. Children as young as 13 work without goggles or safety shields.

"Our main purpose is to develop close feelings toward workers and peasants and let the students get accustomed to manual work," Mr. Ma says.

Chi-mu's and her classmates' courses also have included or will include physics, chemistry, basic agriculture, biology, hygiene, either English or Russian, Chinese language, math, history, geography, revolutionary culture and revolutionary art (painting, drawing and music). Political content is stressed at every opportunity.

In English class, the students practice translating aloud:

"We love our great Socialist motherland."

"Chairman Mao leads us from victory to victory."

"We have a deep love for Chairman Mao."

"He often studies and works late into the night."

Mr. Ma says a second fundamental change since the Cultural Revolution is that more political education is being given to the school's 1,700 students—as is the case throughout China's educational system.

"Our primary task is to train students to be successors to the cause of the proletariat," he says.

Does Chi-mu think Chairman Mao's doctrine is the solution for China's problems or for all countries in the world?

"Mao Tse-tung Thought is a universal truth but must be combined with the conditions and concrete practice of different countries," she replies.

How did she decide that Chairman Mao's doctrine was best? Had she studied other roads to socialism?

"We mainly study the books of Marx, Engels and Lenin and at the same time study the works of Chairman Mao," she says. "I've also read some other books. In history classes my teachers taught us some history of the United States."

Has she ever heard of Thomas Jefferson?

"I read Gorki."

What about Lincoln?

"No."

Washington?

"It has become the capital of the United States."

The third major change in China's schools and universities since the Cultural Revolution has been what Mr. Ma describes as improvements in educational methods. The full educational cycle has been reduced from an average of 17 years to an average of 12.

College study generally has been shortened from four or five years to three. Primary schools have been cut from six years to five. Junior middle schools (junior high schools) now average two years instead of three and senior middle schools (senior high schools) also two years instead of three.

These changes still are in an experimental stage and vary from school to school. At Chi-mu's school, which is both a junior and senior middle school, the junior-high-school course has been left at three years for the time being and the senior-school course cut to two.

She is in the first year of the senior school. When she graduates, she expects to work on a farm or in a factory for two years—a new requirement before anyone will be considered for college—and then, "if I'm needed," she hopes to study to become a teacher.

We meet Chin-hua as he washes his clothes in a wooden tub in the sunshine in front of the cave where he lives in one of the hillsides of Yenan, 420 miles southwest of Peking.

Some 30,000 of the city's 70,000 people live in caves, and many of these dwellings aren't as primitive as they sound. Chin-hua's has walls and a ceiling lined with whitewashed plaster that turns it into a curved-roof vault. The floor is of stone. The entrance is neatly walled up with wood, with a door and a large window in it to admit light.

About a quarter of the cave is occupied by a kang, a large brick bed that is hollow inside to receive the heat from an adjoining stone hearth and in that way keep the sleepers warm in winter. Chin-hua shares the bed with two other young men. Such a setup is considered commodious, for elsewhere families of five or more often share a kang.

He graduated from a junior middle school in Peking in 1970, when most senior middle schools still were closed while reforms were being worked out in the aftermath of the Cultural Revolution. He was sent with seven schoolmates to work in the fields outside Yenan. He says several thousand were sent there from Peking in the two years he has been there.

His mother and father still are in Peking. His father is vice chairman of the revolutionary committee that administers the Chaoyang district of Peking. He sees them once or twice a year on vacations.

Chin-hua knows that everyone must now put in two years of farm or factory work or army service before he can be considered for college. But one gets the impression he would just as soon not make a career of farming.

When is he going to be sent back to Peking he is asked.

"I have no idea."

Would he like to go back?

"Yes." He adds that he would prefer to be a worker in a factory rather than on a farm.

Have his two years here helped him in any way?

"Yes, my attitude has improved here," he says. "Before I came, I didn't know what the peasants were or how hard they had been working or how grain was turned out."

He was given 40 yuan ($17.40) plus food and housing for last year's toil in the fields.

Stroking the long, wispy face hairs that might someday turn into whiskers, Chin-hua contemplates his future with confidence. A white towel is wrapped around his head in traditional peasant fashion. A red Mao badge is pinned to his tunic.

He is confident that he will have a chance to go to college this year or next, he says, because "I'm convinced many people are needed to go to the universities."

As a practical matter, the universities can only accommodate a small percentage of the middle-school graduates who go out each year to work on farms or in factories. One wonders what Chin-hua will be like five or 10 years from now if his hopes should be denied.

No one knows how many young middle-school graduates have been sent from the cities to become peasants.

A foreign-embassy official here says estimates range from 10 million to 20 million or more, with a reduced flow of 400,000 officially reported as having been sent since the beginning of this year.

Of the 1,000 to 2,000 Chinese who flee to Hong Kong each month, most aren't so much hostile to the Communist system as they are disillusioned and personally frustrated at having been sent from the cities to spend their lives as peasants.

Hai-ying wears the green uniform and red insignia of the People's Liberation Army, as do quite a few of the other young men and women at Peking University. He entered in the fall of 1970 when the university reopened after being closed for four years by the tumult of the Cultural Revolution.

His parents both are printers here in Peking. From the time he was two and a half years old until he was seven, they left him in a nursery school six days and nights of every week. He was with them only one day and night on the weekends. This isn't uncommon. Of a small random sampling of parents and children questioned on this subject, roughly 30% had used such boarding nursery schools.

After primary and middle school in Peking, Hai-ying traveled with the Red Guards to Nanking, where he "made propaganda and sang revolutionary songs." After that, he went into the army. He was stationed for slightly over two years in Manchuria.

Harvard-educated Prof. Chou Yi-liang of the Peking University history department contends that the new students coming from the army, farms and factories have much higher comprehensive ability and skill at criticism "than those we had before who left one door of a school and entered another." He adds: "Their thinking processes have been improved; they tend to link theory with practice, and this is a fundamental thing."

The revolution in education is traveling a bumpy road, though. Current enrollment at Peking University is 4,300, up from 2,600 when the school reopened in 1970. But that is a long way from the 8,000 to 10,000 considered normal before the Cultural Revolution. Elsewhere in China, other universities also are reopening and moving back to normal operation with difficulty.

Students with only junior-middle-school (junior-high-school) educations are being admitted and make up more than 60% of the student body at Peking University because so many senior middle schools were closed during the Cultural Revolution and afterward.

And after two years working away from their studies, most entering students require six months of refresher work and senior-middle-school work in the field in which they have been assigned to concentrate. This is provided by the university before they can go into college-level courses.

Hai-ying and other students must meet different entrance requirements from those of the past. First, their parents should be peasants, workers or military personnel; none from a "bourgeois" background are considered.

Then their fellow workers in their farm, factory or army unit must recommend them as having high "political consciousness" as well as academic promise. And the leadership of the commune, factory or army unit must approve. Only then will the application be considered by the university.

These steps are designed to make sure that the educated leaders of tomorrow's China are restricted to the most politically reliable proletarians.

Says Li Chia-kuan, a top member of the revolutionary committee running Peking University: "Before the struggle of the recent Cultural Revolution, whoever got the highest marks got into the school. Now whether you come from a worker or peasant background is important, not marks alone."

Applicants meeting the tests of political reliability were required to pass few if any tests of academic ability when the university reopened in 1970, but now they are given oral and written examinations that are stricter, Mr. Li says. However, because most entering students only have had a junior-high-school education, the entrance exams are geared to that grade level.

Students' tuition, housing and medical expenses are paid by the state, and they get 19.5 yuan ($8.50) a month for meals and pocket money. Food and other costs are much cheaper here than in the U.S.

Once here, the political indoctrination that began in nursery and primary schools continues. Go to any nursery school in China and you will hear the tots shrilly singing songs like this one:

We're called little Red soldiers,

We listen to Chairman Mao's every word.

We want to be revolutionaries even when we're young.

We want to be workers, peasants, soldiers when we're grown up.

Paeans to Chairman Mao and his ideology, and to workers, peasants and soldiers, are integrated into the art, music and other classwork throughout a child's school years and are encountered by him many times a day.

And after college, Hai-ying and others will encounter the same thing many more times a day—on the radio, in the movies and on the stage, in newspapers, on billboards and in required political-discussion sessions lasting several hours a week in whatever farm, factory or army units they spend the rest of their lives.

Will it produce a thoroughly conditioned Pavlovian man, as is often suggested by the uniformity of answers a visitor gets to political or economic questions? Or will the indoctrination pass that perilous point where monotony takes over?

At Peking University, Hai-ying must spend seven hours a week spread over two afternoons or evenings studying Marxism, Leninism and Maoism, with discussion of world affairs included.

"We repudiate such revisionist and bourgeois ideas as studying for oneself and seeking money and fame only for oneself, not for the people," he says.

Seven military men and six factory workers are on the 39-man revolutionary committee that runs the university to make sure the school stays oriented to the masses. A military man is chairman.

Chou Pei-yuan, an American-educated physics professor, who is vice chairman, explains how students of the natural sciences have set up more than 10 small factories and workshops on campus to integrate classroom work with practical experience. One is a small pharmaceutical factory established by biochemistry and organic-chemistry students to make synthesized insulin and medicine to combat intestinal worms. The products are sold to the state pharmaceutical company. Full-time, experienced workers helped them set up the equipment, which was purchased with school funds.

"We cannot establish factories in history, literature and the other liberal arts," Prof. Chou says. "All of society must be their laboratory, their factory. Besides education in basic theory, they must go to the docks, factories, communes, newspapers and army units to do research, to practice writing and to do work among the broad masses of the people. This changes the previous situation, where students were divorced from society. The aim is to train them to be able to analyze and solve problems."

Prof. Chou Yi-liang of the history department worked with his students in a coal mine for three months last year. "We investigated the history of the workers in the mine, their revolutionary history and also the history of the mine in terms of the people's struggle against foreign imperialism," he says.

Students and faculty members are required to do three months of such physical labor a year, two of them integrated with their studies. They also do one day a week of labor in nearby factories or farms or on campus; some are digging air-raid shelters here now.

Seven students sit on the university's revolutionary committee, and Hai-ying believes student participation in running the school is significant.

"We don't criticize our professors, but we help them to remold their outlook," he says. "We have heart-to-heart talks with them over teaching methods—such as cram methods—and over their world outlook. Remolding one's world outlook is a long and heavy task."

Li Chia-kuan of the revolutionary committee says cramming students—"like stuffing a Peking duck"—is one of the "bourgeois methods" eliminated during the Cultural Revolution. "The revisionists wanted to train an intellectual elite, a new mandarin class that thought it was above physical labor and was out of touch with the masses," he says. "The students themselves hadn't been workers or peasants, the teachers separated theory from practice, and they concentrated on cramming students with knowledge without educating them in whom and what it was for."

Lu Ping, president of the university before the Cultural Revolution, was mainly responsible for carrying out this policy on this campus and now is doing punitive physical labor, Mr. Li says. Most of the other 2,000 faculty members were sent to farms for two years of labor and "reeducation" and now have returned, their thinking "remolded."

A principal teaching method currently employed is to print each professor's lecture beforehand for the students to discuss and study among themselves. They prepare questions and bring them to the teacher, who then gives a second lecture based on the problems brought up by the students.

The rewriting of textbooks is another development that resulted from the Cultural Revolution. Part of the purpose is to politicize them. But the basic idea, school administrators say, is to reduce the quantity of material and increase the quality.

A shortening and simplifying effort is being made throughout the educational process at Peking University and elsewhere. The emphasis is on producing not broadly educated young people but politicized specialists.

What was left out when Peking University cut its programs from four or five years to three? "Before the Cultural Revolution, subjects overlapped and were out of date," Mr. Li answers. "There was a lot of repetition in what the students learned, and this made the schooling period longer."

Some think that the shortened, more specialized courses may be just what China needs to turn out large numbers of men and women to help build in a hurry an industrial nation of mostly smaller plants scattered through rural areas. Others argue that lack of depth in education will retard the development of young minds able to deal creatively with their society's problems.

Hai-ying takes a course in the history of the Communist Party and one in world history (from the Communist viewpoint), and the rest of his work is in his English-language specialty.

Peking University doesn't grant degrees anymore, just a certificate. Students who show exceptional talent can be kept at the university for postgraduate work and research in advanced fields. The majority are sent back to the communes or factories or other units from which they came—to help these units with their new expertise.

Hai-ying wants to go back to the People's Liberation Army. "But that's a problem to be decided by the leadership," he says. "I'd like to be an English interpreter or teacher in the PLA."

Students are allowed to express a preference for their field of study and eventual vocation, but the needs of the state come first in deciding what they will do and where in this country they will be assigned to do it.

Whether Hai-ying and his fellow students—particularly the vast majority from rural areas—will get opportunities that will satisfy them, after having seen something of the cities and the larger world outside their villages, is a question for the future, of course.

Farmer Liu's Great Fight

L IU SHU-HSIEN is 56 but looks 70. His face is like the fields he tills: it is deeply furrowed and sun-strengthened and reflects a people and a land mated in adversity long before the fall of Troy.

A few hundred yards from his house, women are picking cotton by hand, others in nearby fields are digging out old corn roots, also by hand, and men are driving oxen pulling wooden plows. This is how it has been through the ages. This Wei River valley was the cradle of Chinese civilization during the Bronze Age. And Sian, 40 miles to the west and now the capital of Shensi Province, was the capital of the Chinese empire from the Chou dynasty in the 11th Century B.C. until the end of the Tang dynasty in A.D. 907.

But there also are some things here now that weren't here before: three red tractors and electric pumps bringing water from wells to irrigate the fields.

These and other changes are responsible for a new optimism in Liu Shu-hsien—an optimism that China will be able to win its race to keep food production rising faster than its growing population. Some 80% of China's 800 million people work on the land and are engaged in this struggle. Food-production figures for the past several years for China as a whole provide grounds for optimism, as they do here in production team No. 1 of the Shuang Wang production brigade of Shuang Wang Commune.

But the problem still is a fundamental one for China and its economy. There are enough uncertainties of man and weather in the future to leave the outcome far from assured.

The late writer Edgar Snow described China's problem in the words the Red Queen used to Alice in "Through the Looking Glass": "Now *here*, you see, it takes all the running you can do, to keep in the same place. If you want to get somewhere else, you must run at least twice as fast as that!"

Every three years China's population grows by the equivalent of France's total population of 50 million. China must run fast indeed to keep output and employment opportunities growing just to prevent a decline in living standards.

And the similarity to Alice's plight doesn't stop there. Because so much of China is mountain and desert, only 11% of its land now is under cultivation, compared with 20% in the U.S. Little additional land in China is suitable to augment this total. And whatever land has been added through irrigation or reclamation projects hasn't offset losses caused by expansion of urban and industrial areas.

Gains in population control are being canceled out, too. The same "barefoot doctors," or paramedical workers, who distribute birth-control advice and contraceptives also provide the rural population generally with inoculations and leadership in sanitation and other public-health measures that are cutting the toll from epidemic diseases and lowering the death rate.

An even more painful dilemma looms for the future: If China is to continue to feed its growing population, it must raise food production partly by mechanizing its agriculture. If millions who now harvest cotton, rice and wheat and weed the fields and apply fertilizer by hand are displaced, as so many American Negroes were in the South, will China's industry have grown enough by then to employ them all?

Liu Shu-hsien is in the front line of the fight to raise food production enough to feed the growing population. He is chairman of the revolutionary committee that runs production team No. 1 here. The team is made up of 103 families with 510 people; that is more than double the size of each of the six other teams in the brigade and the average production team in the country as well.

The Chinese government's strategy, in which Mr. Liu is one of the spear points, includes:

—Use of mass labor to make up for lack of sufficient investment capital and machinery.

—Sharp reduction in the role of the commune in farmers' daily lives; the grant of a large measure of independence to production teams corresponding to the familiar village unit; transmission to farmers of a sense of participation in decisions affecting them; and a compromise with ideology by making sure farmers aren't denied individual material incentives of proven effectiveness.

—Giving priority to modernizing agriculture and investing in industries supporting it, with light industry coming second and heavy industry third—a reversal of the Soviet development pattern.

—Pushing population-limitation measures such as birth control, late marriage and small families.

Manpower and irrigation are what now enable the farmers here at Shuang Wang to harvest two crops of wheat and one of cotton from the same fields each year. On other fields, corn, wheat, onion and cabbage crops all are grown on the same land in a single year.

Some of these crops are planted and growing before the previous crop is harvested. That is possible only because each is picked by hand, not disturbing the new plants, Mr. Liu explains.

One day in 1972, the production team and others in the 20,000-member commune deployed their muscle power to start to reclaim 130 acres of new cropland from part of the now-partially-dry riverbed of the nearby Wei River, a tributary of the Yellow River. They will build dikes to protect the fields to prevent flooding when the river rises and will divert some of the water for irrigation. Forty people a day from this team's 236-person labor force will be assigned to work on the project.

Projects such as this are among the reasons Premier Chou En-lai could predict, in an interview with American editors, that Chinese grain output would exceed 250 million metric tons in 1972 despite the worst drought in nine years. China had given a 1971 figure of 246 million and one for 1970 of 240 million.

Premier Chou's 1972 estimate would be a gain of about 35% from the estimated production of 185 million tons in 1957. That is a shade above the percentage gain that Western analysts figure population registered over the same period.

Today rice and other grains, which bulk large in the Chinese diet, are the only foods besides some oils that are still rationed. But the ration hasn't been restrictive since the early 1960s. And other foods are plentiful.

In Peking, an ambassador from one Western nation says: "Our friends from our embassy in Moscow are all surprised when they visit here at the abundance of the agricultural goods on the market—how much meat, vegetables, fruits are displayed in the shops."

As Liu Shu-hsien sits over his lunch, the adequacy of present food supplies is obvious. And as he begins to describe how his production team operates, it is obvious, too, that farm life has moved a good distance away from earlier efforts to make the commune the principal operating unit, with earnings equalized among commune members and with community mess halls and common ownership of houses and even simple household goods.

Because he has three foreign guests this day, Mr. Liu's wife and youngest daughter, who is 18, have prepared a special meal. The table is laden with plates containing lotus roots, cauliflower and pork, soybean curd noodles and cucumbers, sweet potatoes, scrambled eggs, dumplings of leeks, and cold turnips. A clear whisky distilled from wheat and a sorghum wine are served, too.

If there had been no visitors, the family would have had a regular noon meal of steamed bread or noodles, cabbage or a bean curd dish with a sauce, and eggs.

Mr. Liu explains that he and other members of the production team are paid in food and cash in relation to the number of work points they earn. "The harder you work, the more points you get," he says. "The less work you do, the fewer the points."

But that sounds like a capitalistic system of material incentives, we say. Were we misinformed when we were told one's political attitude was considered in awarding work points?

"Political consciousness isn't an abstract thing," Mr. Liu says. "It's expressed in concrete ways. If you're very active in your work and work very hard and do more work than others, then you will get more work points. But why do you work so well? Obviously it's because you have a high political consciousness."

Behind Mr. Liu's house is a private plot where he grows apples, dates, wheat, cabbages and onions for his family's use and for sale. He also raises his own pigs and chickens. About 5% of the production team's 102 acres are in private plots.

The commune here and elsewhere has evolved into

an administrative unit similar to a local government body. Mr. Liu's commune operates four high schools, a hospital and several light-industrial plants from which it finances its own operations. The production brigades run 13 primary schools, a flour mill, an iron works, a farm-implement plant, a clothes-making shop and a motor-repair facility.

Decisions on many farming matters and almost all labor questions are left basically to the individual production teams to work out independently. Team No. 1 —which is the same as saying the villagers of Shuang Wang—gave 34% of its gross income last year to its production brigade for chemical fertilizer, insecticides and fungicides, other production supplies, farm-implement depreciation, gas and other maintenance and taxes. It set aside another 7% in an accumulation fund for welfare expenses and capital construction and allotted 20% of this to the brigade to finance projects from which the team benefits.

The rest of the production team's income was divided among its members according to the number of work points earned during the year. If one production team has more productive land or works harder and produces more than neighboring teams, it has a bigger melon to slice up among its members. More prosperous teams need not share with poorer teams—and this lack of egalitarianism provides a further incentive to members of a village to work hard.

A sense of personal participation is cultivated to further fuel the feeling that members are working for themselves. "Everyone sits down and discusses how many work points cotton picking should be worth," Mr. Liu says. "Then you get the work points according to how many baskets you picked."

Production quotas and capital-investment decisions are other matters discussed at meetings down at the production-team level.

In 1971, Mr. Liu's team produced 243 tons of grain in addition to other crops, and it expects 1972 grain output to be about 260 tons. The average 1971 net income for each person in the team, he figures, was the yuan equivalent of about $292, of which $122 was payable in grain, plus about another $72 per person from the private family plots.

This income can't easily be gauged in American terms because prices of food, medical care and other goods and services are much lower here. Even allowing that the villagers' standard of living is low by U.S. yardsticks, Mr. Liu believes that he and his fellow townsmen are doing fine, particularly when they compare their lives today with past years.

"Members of our production team have 73 bicycles, 22 sewing machines and over 30 radios," he says, rattling off the symbols by which most of China seems to measure personal affluence these days. "About 80% of the families have watches or clocks or both. About 70% have some savings in the bank."

He says each family has built a new house since 1954. His own, in which he has lived with seven other members of his family for 14 years, is about average. A one-story house, it is made of brick, with the walls plastered with dried mud mixed with straw. The walls are painted white inside and are decorated with photos of Mao Tse-tung and colored pictures of Peking Opera scenes clipped from magazines. The roof is tile.

There are two bedrooms equipped with kangs, the traditional rural beds made of brick and hollow inside, with a built-in hearth for keeping the brick and the sleeper warm in winter. There also are a kitchen, with a table and a brick hearth, and a large center hall, between the front and rear doors, that serves as a dining area and is equipped with a wooden table and four small unpainted wood benches. In the kitchen and dining area stand three waist-high earthenware jars in which grain is stored.

To the rear of the house are a water pump and outside privy. In front is a courtyard enclosed by a wall. Clusters of corn hang from the trees, drying in the sun.

The farmers' homes here in Shuang Wang and other rural areas visited during 24 days in China generally were roomier than the workers' housing seen in the cities. Unlike the farmers, the workers cannot own their own homes; they rent from the state or their factory. Most workers' families visited were squeezed into one or two rooms and shared kitchen and toilet facilities with other families.

Before the Communists came to power, "I was a hired hand and had never been to school," recalls Mr. Liu, who has lived in this village all his life. "Now I've been to literacy classes in the village and can read the newspaper. Before liberation, we lived in a very small hut. It has collapsed now. We only had grain for half a year; after that we ate husks and roots. There were 46 households here then, and seven families died of starvation between 1929 and 1949."

To keep food production rising ahead of population growth, the government is encouraging counties and communes to build plants that make irrigation pumps and to build fertilizer factories, farm-implement plants and other agriculture-related industries. These are to be built in the midst of the farming areas, not in the cities.

The purposes are several: to create jobs in the country and prevent urban congestion; to draw on local investment funds and spare the central government's resources for heavier industry; to make farmers more willing to make such investments by letting them observe at first hand how the local plants benefit them directly; and to save overburdening the country's transportation network. Another purpose—and not the least important—is to engage local farm people in manufacturing. This would be another step toward removing apathy and ignorance and substituting more modern, technically oriented attitudes that can provide the ground in which modernization will flourish best.

Alva Lewis Erisman, a U.S. government China specialist, made the following estimates of progress toward modernization in a study prepared for Congress:

Tractor production rose from 1,000 conventional tractors in 1958 to 28,000 conventional units in 1971 and 22,000 small garden tractors that are operated by a man steering them while walking behind. Many production lines for the latter are housed in small local plants.

Chemical-fertilizer production, measured in standard units of fixed nutrient content such as nitrogen or phosphorus, rose from 803,000 metric tons in 1957 to 7.4 million in 1970. The small plants' share of nitrogen-fertilizer output is estimated to be one-third. China still applies only one-tenth the fertilizer per unit of land as do West European countries and Japan.

Mechanical pumps for irrigation were produced to the tune of 700,000 horsepower in 1957, and eight million horsepower by 1966. And the capacity of pumps produced for farms in 1971 was reported equal to more than one-sixth the capacity of all pumps produced between 1949 and 1969.

China had turned about 2.6 million acres into high-yield cropland by 1957 as a result of controlled irrigation and drainage. This rose to only three million acres by 1963 but then leaped to 5.2 million by 1971—double the area in 1957.

Output gains in farm equipment and supplies have been one contributor to industrial-production gains estimated by the Central Intelligence Agency at 12% last year and another 12% for the first half of 1972, compared with a year earlier.

The gains of recent years have more than offset declines in gross national product (excluding services) during the 1958-1968 period, giving China a long-term growth rate of 4%. Since population has been expanding about 2% a year, a gradual improvement in living standards has been made possible.

Alexander Eckstein, a University of Michigan professor, who specializes in China's economy, calls the 4% growth rate "quite impressive" by the long-term historical standards of present industrialized countries; it is about the same as the long-term rate of expansion in Japan from the time it began industrializing at the end of the last century.

This may augur well for China's long-term prospects, compared with those of other developing nations such as India. But because the growth rates of many industrialized societies such as Japan are above 4% today, the economic gap between them and China may widen rather than narrow in the future even as China moves ahead.

Here in Shensi Province, as elsewhere throughout China, population-control efforts are being pressed to try to keep total production gains from failing to result in maximum per-capita gains.

Yang Hsiao-ping, a female member of the province's family-planning committee, says that free contraceptives are distributed and that every neighborhood committee or commune family-planning committee works to "educate" young people to wait until they are in their late twenties before marrying and then to limit themselves to two children.

Are choice job assignments, educational opportunities or larger housing withheld from those who don't comply, as a means to induce cooperation? "No," Mrs.

Yang says, "but there is public opinion. If everyone conducts family planning and one has too many children, public opinion will be against him. Even the neighbors wouldn't think it a good thing if you had too many children."

However, birth-control education is being carried out among the peasants by the paramedical workers, who are improving general medical care and sanitation at the same time, thereby reducing mortality rates.

Largely for this reason, John S. Aird, a U.S. authority on China's population, found that four statistical projections of China's population to 1990, using different assumptions and variables each time, resulted in a range of only 1,319,000,000 to 1,330,000,000.

New Man, New Religion

CHINA'S effort to create a "new Maoist man" is producing a paradox of success amidst failure.

The goal of this human-engineering experiment on one-fourth of the world's population is a citizenry dedicated to working only for the good of society and the state, not for personal material rewards or career gains. To most Americans, this attempt to remold 800 million minds would seem an Orwellian experiment in changing human nature itself. For despite the debates of philosophers through the centuries over the nature of man, history provides scant evidence that selflessness is a durable human quality.

The Chinese leaders are recognizing this, too. While professing hope for the future, they are backpedaling from idealism today. Material incentives are widely denounced—and just as widely employed. Most farm and factory workers' earnings are tied closely to how hard each individual works. And alongside the carrot there remains the stick: The political and social pressure for conformity to the "Maoist man" vision is powerful and pervasive.

Even so, the idea of the "new man," putting service to the collective before self, has a power in China that should not be underestimated. That's partly because China's cultural and historical heritage is worlds removed from the Western experience, and partly because the "new man" concept is identified with patriotism, nationalism and an improved life. The result is that it is successfully serving an important function for China's leaders: It is helping to provide a sense of purpose cementing together much of this vast and diverse country.

No foreign visitor can gauge how much of the support of the selfless-service doctrine represents consensus, how much conformity. He can only recount his impressions—impressions measured against those of diplomats long resident here and of expatriate Chinese who had mingled with friends and relatives on visits here.

The impression one carries away is that China may never attain Mao's ideal of "spiritual transformation" of its vast population, any more than Western man succeeds in daily attaining the ideals of the Ten Commandments. But even while compromising between hard reality and the Utopian "new man" vision, much of China appears to be accepting it in principle as a new social philosophy and code of values to aspire to—a state religion.

The rhetoric of service is pervasive. Ask Chiang Yun-hsiang, an official of the Tien Shan Street Committee, which administers a section of Shanghai holding 74,000 people, what her 12 nurseries teach their 2,-000 toddlers. "How best to serve the people when they grow up," she answers.

Or ask Shi Ar-chen, a retired textile worker here, what her hopes are for her four grandchildren. "That they might serve the people according to the needs of our state," comes the reply.

The same question is asked of Tin Shu-chen, wife of a worker in an electric power plant, about her four children, and she answers, "To listen to Chairman Mao and do what the state needs."

It doesn't take long for the answers to these and

other questions to become predictable. Push the right button and out comes the learned, programmed response.

Wei Shu-ling, chairman of the revolutionary committee that runs the Peking Arts and Crafts Factory, proclaims: "Here the workers' enthusiasm is to build socialism for the collective, and not for himself." Tien Yu-ling, a design technician at the plant, says: "Chairman Mao taught me to know I am serving the people."

It would be naive, of course, to translate the mouthing of party-line cliches at showplace communes and factories into evidence of wide popular support. It must be weighed along with observation of the spirit of the people encountered at random elsewhere, and with China's culture and historical experience.

The American doctrine of individualism and individual freedom is alien to the Chinese experience, and almost incomprehensible to them. Their tradition is one of mutual dependence; the focus of their society, their duties and obligations since Confucian times was the family and various extensions of the family such as the clan and village.

The Chinese tradition, Harvard historian John King Fairbank has written, was "that the acts of a person were to be judged mainly by their contribution to social welfare and stability. The individual as such was not exalted. . . . Emphasis upon individual self-expression tended too often toward license and anarchy, and so the Chinese tradition emphasized social conduct."

When individual interests always were subordinated to kinship and communal loyalties, it is not an impossible leap to subordinate them instead to a production team or some other present-day communal unit, particularly when this unit largely has replaced the family as the primary source of security.

A national social consciousness and civic sense was

more alien to Chinese tradition. Yet even that is being aroused with considerable success.

That's partly a product of improved literacy, modern communications, educational indoctrination, social pressure and party organization at the grass roots. But most important, it is a product of patriotic pride in China's achievements.

Peasants, students, factory workers and others feel their country stands independent and self-confident in the world today, in contrast to its weakness and humiliations in the century after the Opium War. Its people have low living standards by American measurements, but at least a security from hopeless poverty that they did not have in the past, particularly in the chaotic decades of civil war, war with Japan, inflation, epidemics and famine that preceded the Communist seizure of power in 1949.

Now, especially with the disorders of the Cultural Revolution behind them, the Chinese are enjoying "the pleasure that comes from subsidizing pain," as one foreign diplomat puts it. All this has brought the ordinary citizen a new sense of national dignity and self-respect.

Says a Western ambassador with long service in China: "The government has removed the fear of want and the terrible uncertainty—not knowing whether you would starve, or lose your home, or freeze in the winter."

"How can you disagree with those who have accomplished so much?" is a question the Chinese put to skeptics. Millions of Chinese thus appear willing to put their faith in the regime, not because of its Communist ideology but because it has bettered their lives and they look to it as the means to further improvements. For them, so far, the line has been thin between the pursuit of individual self-interest, which is condemned, and the identification of their material self-interest with acceptance of the government and its philosophy of the collective, an identification China's leaders naturally try to encourage.

Chan Kui-yun is a worker in Textile Factory No. 4 in Sian, the capital of Shensi Province. Her mother and father were textile workers before her. She's 42 and has been working in mills since she was 14. She, her husband and three children live crowded into two gloomy rooms, sharing a kitchen and bathroom with another family.

"Your life is basically the same as it always has been, isn't it?" she is asked.

"No," she says. "I used to work 12 hours a day, we lived in misery and we had nothing. Today I have everything I'd want—a bicycle, a clock, even a sewing machine. I had no political status. After Liberation we stood up."

Pride in achievements at the local level often are as strong a force as national pride. Wei Juin-tai, 70, and other members of the Ta Tsai Yuan production brigade of the Cheng Kuang Commune, in Linhsien County of Honan Province, talk most about the way irrigation from the Red Flag Canal they helped to build has raised yields of wheat and corn, enabled them to plant two crops a year and bettered their lives.

Resistance to total implementation of the vision of selflessness is best seen at the local level, too. When the farm communes first were set up in 1958, efforts were made to institute common ownership of homes and even household goods, equality of pay, free and equal food for all, even common dining halls and dormitories in some cases. All these notions had to be abandoned.

The commune is today a local governing unit, exercising administrative powers, running affiliated light industries and health and education facilities. But the production team, a unit of sometimes 30, sometimes as many as 100 families corresponding to the former village, has been turned into the basic economic unit. The more the production team produces, the more its members have to divide among themselves (after deducting contributions to the state, to communal investment funds and for seed and other supplies). No longer is there talk of the more productive production teams sharing with their less productive neighbors in the commune to equalize compensation.

Small private family plots and family ownership of small numbers of pigs and other livestock were loudly condemned during the 1966-69 Cultural Revolution, but were never eliminated lest peasant motivation and morale be weakened. These plots make up an estimated 5% to 7% of commune land.

The computation of earnings for farm and factory workers also shows clearly that the pursuit of material self-interest is far from dead in this country—and that the regime recognizes this and believes it must adapt to it to motivate its citizens.

Farm pay is determined by a system of work points awarded largely on the basis of how much a person produces. Mao Shu-ying, the 19-year-old daughter of one of Mr. Wei's neighbors in Ta Tsai Yuan, in Honan Province, says work points are awarded on the basis of "attitude toward labor, how hard the work is and a person's skill."

When asked to elaborate, she adds: "If one person picks 10 baskets of cotton or corn and someone else picks 15, the one who picks 15 gets more points. That's because he shows more skill and also a better attitude to labor."

Conversations with farm production team leaders and factory managers elsewhere leave no doubt this prevails generally. And this individual material reward is not unimportant in keeping the economy's wheels turning.

Wei Shu-ling, chairman of the revolutionary committee that manages the Peking Arts and Crafts Factory, which turns out lacquerware, cloissone items and other art products, tells how there are eight different pay grades at her plant, and a worker's classification and salary depends on his "ability and the length of time he has worked."

"Ability and political consciousness are a unified whole," she says. "If you love socialism and want to contribute the most to socialism, you will try very hard and do your work well." In other words, she acknowledges, ability means volume of work turned out as well as quality, and that's what counts in setting pay.

At a small factory in Shanghai that's run by the Tien Shan Street Committee, and where neighborhood women work full-time producing handkerchiefs and embroidery work for export, officials freely admit workers are paid piece rates.

There are different types of incentives within the system here that encourage political conformity, too. Correct ideological attitudes are among the considerations in awarding job assignments, promotions, educational opportunities, housing accommodations—and social approval.

And if the carrot doesn't work, the stick is there, too, to induce conformity by those who question the new faith, or at least the way it is practiced.

Under the street committees are neighborhood or lane committees, and there are comparable smaller groupings in factories, farm communes, schools and other organizations. They are responsible for street cleaning and public health measures in the case of the neighborhood committees, various operating functions in the other cases—and the neighbors' ideology in both.

This system of surveillance and coercion predates the Communists; it showed up during the Sung dynasty in the 11th Century and the Manchus and Nationalists employed it, too. Dissenters face the penalties of social ostracism or public recantation.

If they persist, they can be shipped off to compulsory "reeducation through labor" of the punitive variety, as opposed to the periods of farm or factory work many city dwellers routinely put in nowadays as part of the campaign to blur the distinctions between mental and manual work. This penalty can be invoked if the person's organization expels him for "violating discipline" or "refusing to be directed in production work" —work of a sort and at a location over which he has no control, of course.

"The effectiveness of the regime's propaganda and indoctrination efforts is clearly reinforced by the population's realization that non-conformity may be interpreted as a sign of political dissidence," A. Doak Barnett, a leading China scholar who is affiliated with the Brookings Institution, has written, "and any signs of the latter are likely to invoke suppression by the apparatus of police control."

No one can say with certainty how much of the support of the regime and its Maoist philosophy derives from faith, how much from fear. For now, there appears to be a sufficient sense of progress to make most Chinese willing adherents of the new Maoist religion, if they are allowed to practice it with moderation—and to make the concept of the "new man serving the people" a strong unifying force useful to the state.

For the future, will the ceaseless indoctrination of the young be enough to offset their lack of experience with pre-Communist deprivation with which to compare their own lives? Will they become part of the revolution of rising expectations?

The answer lies with how successful China's next generation of leaders will be in feeding, employing and improving the lives of their steadily growing population. The future of China—and of the "new Maoist man" idea—will hang more on such material considerations than on ideological persuasiveness.

Winds of Change

CHILDREN'S toys and comic books are being studied in China as clues to the development of more relaxed Chinese domestic and foreign policies.

The toy attracting the most attention is a little stuffed tiger with the word "Wong" on its forehead. Wong means king—king of the animals. This is a traditional Chinese toy once believed to ward off evil spirits.

The comic book is a child's version of "The Monkey King," a tale of an adventurous monk's travels in the seventh century. It is a classic written by Wu Cheng-en in the 16th century.

Both items vanished from store shelves during the 1966-1969 Cultural Revolution's attacks on everything old from the days of "feudal" or "bourgeois" society. They have just been put on sale again. "The Monkey King" is the first classic republished since the Cultural Revolution.

Other changes, both major and minor, reflect the trend toward more moderate policies. And the policies, in turn, reflect growing confidence by the Chinese that both at home and abroad events are moving in their favor. They also reflect decisions by the men in power to try to be more practical after the doctrinaire excesses during the Cultural Revolution and in its wake.

Here are a few of the other straws in the wind:

Junior Foreign Ministry officials are accepting invitations to dinner at the homes of junior diplomats from some foreign embassies and are staying until midnight. Such socializing was unheard of up to 1972.

Kung Chen, a 26-year-old art historian at the Forbidden City's Manchu palaces, reports that a magazine on archeology resumed publication this year and that books on archeology are back in the stores—both after a six-year suspension. The Forbidden City itself was closed from 1966 until 1970 as part of the campaign against old things.

Frances and Richard Hadden, an American piano duo, gave a two-hour concert before an audience of 600 here in early October 1972. It was called "From Bach to Rock and Back." It was the first public performance of Western music since before the Cultural Revolution. Mrs. Hadden, the daughter of the former Episcopal bishop of Hangchow, had known Premier Chou En-lai in China before World War II.

An Englishman was seated in a park recently when a Chinese student of English struck up a conversation with him. "Are you allowed to talk to Chinese?" the boy asked. "Yes," he was told. "Are you allowed to talk to foreigners?" The boy replied, "We didn't used to be, but we are now."

On a much more significant plane, the role of the People's Liberation Army, or PLA, in running the country is receding slightly. The army still is a major force, of course; PLA men hold about half the seats on the Communist Party Central Committee and the Politburo. In the provinces, over half the chairmen of the governing revolutionary committees and the leaders of the provincial Communist Party hierarchy are army men. They also still hold the chairmanship of the revolutionary committees that run many of the nation's institutions.

A sampling of how they still permeate the nation's life: Wang Lien-lung, chairman of the revolutionary

All photographs, unless otherwise noted, were taken by Warren Phillips of The Wall Street Journal.

left:
A pigtailed child clutches a small doll as she sits pensively in a communal nursery in Sian. The nursery is operated by Textile Factory No.4 for children of workers.

below:
A view of Peking's Chang An avenue, with Tien An Men Square and the Great Hall of the People in the rear center of the photograph.

left:
Pu Chao-min of China's Hsinhua news agency poses in Yenan with an old worker who had known Chairman Mao Tse-tung in the 1940s. The man wears a Mao medal and a white towel, typical peasant headgear.

below:
Author Warren Phillips joins a group of youngsters on a hillside road near Yenan in north central China, a Communist stronghold during China's civil war.

above: Pedaling down a rain-slicked boulevard, work-bound bicyclists pay little heed to a heroic worker's billboard on the roadside. (photo by John Duprey, New York Daily News)

below: A close-up view of the Gate of Heavenly Peace from Tien An Men Square.

right:
Premier Chou En-lai, 74, gestures as he talks with a delegation of 22 American editors during an interview in the Great Hall of the People in Peking.
(photo by John Duprey, New York Daily News)

below:
The Great Wall snakes over rugged mountain terrain. The fortification, about 1,400 miles long, on the northern and northwestern border of China proper, dates in original form from the Third Century B.C.
(photo by John Duprey, New York Daily News)

left:
A girl intently uses a small drill to carve a piece of ivory in the Arts and Crafts Factory in Peking.

below:
The words of a popular children's song are written in English on a blackboard at Middle School No. 31 in Peking for the benefit of visiting American editors.

left:
High school students doing calisthenics en masse at Middle School No. 31 in Peking.

below:
When planes are delayed at Peking's airport, airport staff members soothe the stalled passengers with revolutionary music, performed on ancient instruments.
(photo by Anne Keatley)

right:
Mao Tsai-chin, a 50-year-old farm worker's wife, and her child peer at the camera in the commune where they live in Linhsien County, Honan Province.

below:
A view from the sixth floor of the Peking Hotel looking into the courtyards of homes near the hotel.

left:
Two members of the militia take rifle training in a dry river bed outside Yenan.

below:
Four young members of the Red Guards display their red armbands at Peking's Middle School No. 31. On the far right is Wang Chi-mu, 17, who is profiled in Chapter III.

大海航行靠舵手 干革命靠毛泽东思想

全世界无产者联合起来！

above: A poster of Chairman Mao looms over a literature class in a junior Middle School near Peking. (photo by Anne Keatley)

below: Surgeons in Capital Hospital in Peking prepare to give woman patient acupuncture anesthesia prior to a thyroid tumor operation.
(Copyright 1972, The Oklahoma Publishing Co.)

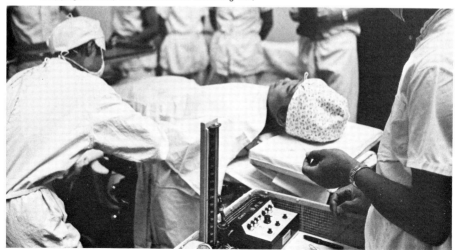

right:
Worker displays a string of fresh-water oysters in which pearls are cultivated at a commune in Wuhsi, a bit north and west of Shanghai. (Copyright 1972, The Oklahoma Publishing Co.)

below:
Fish farmers net a nice harvest from one of the many fish ponds in the Wuhsi area.

above: A carrier totes a couple of loads of gravel as laborers toil on building a new street in Linshien County.

below: Manpower remains the most common way of moving materials in China. Here, at a construction site in Yenan, workers haul a hefty load of timbers up a dirt road.

right:
In the ages old manner, a woman washes her clothes—and her feet—in a shallow stream near Yenan.

below:
An ox drags a man atop a primitive harrow to pulverize and smooth soil in a field at the Shuang Wang Commune east of Sian.

left:
Cave houses, common in the Yenan area, are dug into the sides of the hills and provide compact but relatively comfortable living places. (Copyright 1972, The Oklahoma Publishing Co.)

below:
An apartment dweller in Shanghai in a rather typical kitchen. Usually, kitchens are shared by two to four families. (Copyright 1972, The Oklahoma Publishing Co.)

right:
Water carried through nearby mountains by a laboriously constructed canal system rushes into once-barren Linhsien County in Honan Province.

below:
Corn shelling down on the commune is usually a family affair, with even the youngest helping out. (Copyright 1972, The Oklahoma Publishing Co.)

left:
Markets are well stocked with meat, fish, and vegetables at low prices. At this one in Peking, the poster of Mao reminds shoppers of whence the goods came.
(photo by Anne Keatley)

below:
A market in Shanghai offers a wide variety of fowl and vegetables.

left:
Laughing children do a folk
dance at National Day celebra-
tions at the Summer Palace
outside of Peking. Formerly
a country retreat for China's
emperors, the place is now a
public park.

below:
Picturesque and practical,
those boats and fishermen
on an outlet of Lake Taihu
near Wuhsi help supply food
for China's millions.
(Copyright 1972, The Oklahoma
Publishing Co.)

committee that directs Peking University, is an army
man, and six other PLA men sit with him on the 39-
member committee. Also a PLA man is the chairman of
the revolutionary committee of the Shensi Province
Song and Dance Ensemble and the Shensi Song and
Dance School. There are four army men on the 27-man
revolutionary committee running Textile Factory No. 4
in the city of Sian. The number hasn't changed since
1970, when it was raised from two.

On the other hand, Premier Chou is gradually
trying to reduce the PLA role in civilian affairs and
turn them back to party control. Diplomats here believe
that this was partly responsible for precipitating the
showdown with former Defense Minister Lin Piao. Mr.
Lin was Chairman Mao Tse-tung's chosen successor
until Mr. Lin was killed while allegedly trying to flee
the country after an unsuccessful attempt to seize
power.

The nation's civilian militia, which was removed
from army control in September 1971, the time of the
Lin Piao crisis, was quietly put under the command of
Communist Party officials in June 1972.

At the Peking Arts and Crafts Factory, which turns
out jade and ivory carvings and other artworks, there
was a PLA man on the 13-member revolutionary committee, but he left early in 1972. There are two army
men on the 18-man revolutionary committee of Peking's
Middle School No. 31, down from three at the end of
1971.

"The army was needed to administer many institutions that were disrupted by the Cultural Revolution,
but now it has accomplished its task," one government
official says.

The people used to be urged to "Learn from the
Army." Now the army is being urged to "Learn from the

People." In China, changes like that are never made casually.

Signs of a return to normality show up in other sectors of the domestic scene. Party officials, managers, technicians and others purged at the time of the Cultural Revolution are reappearing in increasing numbers in positions of responsibility. Among those who resurfaced in the summer of 1972 were Chen Yun, formerly Peking's top economic planner and a Politburo member, and Chen Tsai-tao, the former military commander for central China. He collaborated in a rebellion against the extremist Red Guards and the central government in the industrial city of Wuhan in 1967.

On the farms and in factories, there is fresh emphasis on tying pay to how hard a person works rather than to his political fervor. And more and more universities are reopening after being closed four or more years. Entrance examinations are being reintroduced and stiffened after a period of choosing students almost solely on the ground of political reliability with little regard for academic ability.

In foreign affairs, the 1972 visit by President Nixon was the most spectacular reflection of changing policy. It is being followed by an increasing U.S.-Chinese exchange of doctors, scientists, athletes, newsmen and others.

In a meeting with a delegation from the American Society of Newspaper Editors at the offices of the People's Daily, the Communist Party's newspaper, Vice Editor Chen Chun refers to the "beneficial results" growing out of the Nixon trip. He adds: "To give you a very good example, isn't it beneficial that the gentlemen here participating in the discussions today can come to China?"

What accounts for the Chinese confidence that events at home and abroad are moving in their favor?

In October 1972, West Germany and Japan

brought to 80 the number of countries having diplomatic relations with the People's Republic of China.
Recognition was granted by more than 20 nations in
1972 alone after Peking replaced Taiwan in the United
Nations. All this weakens the Chiang Kai-shek government on Taiwan by increasing its diplomatic isolation.

At home, industrial production rose an estimated
18% in 1970 and 12% in 1971; Western intelligence
sources estimate it was up another 12% in the first half
of 1972 from a year earlier. There have been good grain
crops for several years, too; Chinese officials say irrigation progress helped offset drought in parts of the nation in 1972.

There also seems to be greater domestic stability
for the moment than there has been in several years.
Both the convulsions of the Cultural Revolution and
Lin Piao's ill-starred bid for power are out of the way
now. "People in the government seem more relaxed now
that the purges of Lin Piao's followers are over," one
foreign diplomat says.

The more moderate policies are probably most
closely related to domestic developments. But, perhaps
not incidentally, they also have a design overseas: to
project the image of a more relaxed, stable and respectable China. In this way, Peking's influence in Asia and
the world might be enhanced, and the obstacles to its
claim to Taiwan might be reduced.

If the Chinese are brimming over with confidence
these days because they see brighter prospects on the
foreign and domestic fronts, that doesn't mean they are
without their serious problems. The biggest question
mark is who will succeed the 78-year-old Chairman
Mao, the 74-year-old Premier Chou and other members
of the aging leadership.

Foreign diplomats here figure that the 21-member
Politburo has been reduced to ten because of ousters

during the Cultural Revolution and during the Lin Piao affair as well as because of natural deaths. There were five members of the standing committee of the Politburo, and three are gone, leaving only Mr. Mao and Mr. Chou. Many ministerial posts, including that of defense minister, and many seats on the Central Committee also have been open a year or more.

The fact that they have been empty so long indicates to China scholars in the diplomatic community that power blocs in the country—the party bureaucracy, the army and various provincial leaders—haven't been able to reach agreement on how much authority will be exercised by each and to agree on replacements to fill the empty jobs.

"The problem of the succession is still open and set in dramatic terms," one diplomat says. "At the time of Stalin's death a collective leadership was formed because several people were necessary to fill the vacuum left by Stalin. But at that time the Soviet Union had the frames of power working normally. Chou En-lai has indicated China will react with collective leadership at the time of Mao's death. But if you take the hypothesis of Mao's dying tomorrow, neither the party nor the state is reconstructed in its normal frame. Both have to be rebuilt. It's very dangerous."

While China struggles with this problem, its moves toward more moderation in domestic and foreign policies are being widely interpreted as changes in tactics, not in strategic goals.

In foreign affairs, China's aim still is to extend its influence and ideology in Asia and the world. It seeks to do this by the attraction of the Maoist political philosophy and by uniting with third-world nations and other countries to try to reduce the influence of the U.S. and Russia. The budding rapprochement with the U.S. is designed to counter the Soviet threat, hasten the absorption of Taiwan and speed the reduction of the American military presence on China's southern and eastern frontiers.

At home, the goal also remains unchanged, even if the methods for reaching it are being altered. The goal is the building of a China with a much more modern agricultural and industrial base within a society stressing collective efforts and aspirations rather than individual freedom and rewards.

The Cultural Revolution, one of the great upheavals of history, was not only a power struggle between Chairman Mao and Liu Shao-chi, then chief of state; it was also a struggle over basic policy. Mr. Mao felt that Mr. Liu's policies in the party, the government bureaucracy, the schools and the economy were leading to rule by an urban-based managerial and professional elite, preoccupied with its careers and privileges and out of touch with the farm and factory laborers. He had seen this happen in Russia and didn't want to take the same "revisionist, capitalist-road" course.

He turned loose the nation's youth, the Red Guards from the high schools and colleges, to destroy the party, government and educational bureaucracies. He hoped to rekindle in the youth the revolutionary zeal of the past and rebuild the country on more egalitarian lines. Other Cultural Revolutions may be needed in the future, Chairman Mao has warned.

After two years of tumult, the army was called in to restore order and lead the country back from chaos. Now, as many of the people and practices denounced during the Cultural Revolution are restored to legitimacy, the question arises: Was the Cultural Revolution such a fiasco that Chairman Mao has been forced to retreat from it? Or did the extremist policies of that period accomplish what he wanted, permitting a return now to normality and the rebuilding of a society without some of the Cultural Revolution's excesses?

The Chinese say the latter is the case. They talk of the Cultural Revolution's achievements and speak of it as something that still is proceeding in many respects. Foreign experts split on the question, with a great many taking the former view.

What can be said with certainty is that despite the return of some of the people and policies that the Cultural Revolution attacked, it has left an imprint on Chinese society that won't soon fade.

The state bureaucracy and that of individual institutions have been cut drastically. Foreign authorities on China report that, compared with the period before the Cultural Revolution, the number of state ministries in Peking and their manpower levels "seem to have been reduced by about half." An ambassador here with long experience in China says his staff has observed that this streamlining has produced a notable efficiency.

In the provinces and at many factories and other organizations, the story is the same. Keng Chi-chang, vice chairman of the revolutionary committee that administers Honan Province, says the committee's personnel has been cut by two-thirds.

"We simplified the routine work, got rid of all the duplication and overlap of agencies, and improved our efficiency and heightened our political consciousness," he says. Different bureaus had separate office buildings in the provincial capital of Chengchou before the Cultural Revolution but now are consolidated in one building, he adds. "And we still have more room in our offices than before," he says.

Bureaucrats also may be slower than before in seeking privileges and perquisites or showing attitudes of "elitism" or "careerism" when they think back upon the viciousness of the attacks on these practices and attitudes during the Cultural Revolution.

Factory managers in Shanghai, Sian and elsewhere are living in the same housing accommodations as their workers, doing without cars for personal use and spending a day a week on the production line. Government officials and college faculty members spend a portion of each year at farms, where they haul manure and work the fields to "reintegrate with the masses." All in all, egalitarianism has been reinforced, at least for now.

The "Maoist-man" concept of selfless "service to the people" and the state, rather than pursuit of personal rewards, also has been promoted more strongly since the Cultural Revolution.

And the Cultural Revolution's impact on the educational system has been striking. Political indoctrination has been stepped up. Academic work is being compressed and mixed vigorously with labor and practical experience, through the introduction of industrial workshops at most schools and the requirement that students spend part of each year working on a farm commune or in a factory.

Correct political attitudes are a much more important consideration in accepting candidates for college. Other new requirements are that a high-school graduate have worked two years on a farm or in a factory since graduation and that his parents have a "proletarian background."

After Mao, What?

PREMIER Chou En-lai said in effect that a collective leadership will succeed to power in China after Mao Tse-tung passes from the scene.

There had been speculation in the West that this would be so, but no official word from the Chinese government until now. The confirmation came in a statement by Mr. Chou that the "naming of only one successor was one of the plots of Lin Piao." The government has said that Lin, who was defense minister and Mr. Mao's designated successor, tried unsuccessfully to seize power in September of 1971 and was killed while trying to flee the country.

"With such a big country and the problems facing us, how can you have only one successor?" Mr. Chou asked.

In the course of the three-hour-and-40-minute conversation, Mr. Chou also disclosed:

—The government expects food-grain output in 1972 to exceed 250 million metric tons, despite what he called more natural calamities, mainly drought, than China had experienced in the preceding nine years. China claimed production of 246 million metric tons in 1971 and 240 million in 1970. (A metric ton is 2,204.6 pounds.)

—In 1958, Nikita Khrushchev, then Soviet premier, proposed setting up a joint navy with China. Chairman

Mao, sensing a Russian desire to control China's fleet, refused.

—China wants no part of any industrial-development joint ventures with American companies, similar to those negotiated in East Europe and elsewhere. Experience in joint ventures with the Soviet Union soured China on such deals, he said.

—Chairman Mao overrode the premier in extending the 1971 invitation to the United States Ping-Pong team that led to efforts to achieve a rapprochement between China and the United States. (Whether Mr. Chou's story of this incident was merely intended to show the customary deference to Chairman Mao as the principal source of wisdom in China wasn't clear.)

—He is convinced the identity of the "principal culprit, the man who planned the assassination" of President Kennedy has never been divulged. "It couldn't be" that Lee Harvey Oswald is "the one who really killed him," Mr. Chou said firmly. "It is not possible."

China's premier met with American editors in a reception room in the Great Hall of the People. Also present were Assistant Foreign Minister Chang Wen-chin and leaders of the Chinese press. Mr. Chou, obviously in good spirits, set a tone that seemed designed to project a picture of a China that was relaxed, stable, and sure of itself and had its major problems well in hand.

He ranged at length over such diverse topics as the grooming of future leaders, relations with the United States, China's economic priorities, Chairman Mao's philosophy, Russian shortcomings, his own enjoyment of Ping-Pong as a source of relaxation, future pollution problems and New York traffic.

Flashes of wit were frequent. A few samples:

—While he said he was precluded from visiting the United States as China's premier so long as the Chiang Kai-shek government had representatives in America, "if I resigned, maybe I could go. Maybe I'll go as a member of the table tennis team."

—Noting that The New York Times, The Washington Post and certain other newspapers weren't represented in the visiting editors group, he said: "But The Wall Street Journal is represented. Last time you didn't come, but someone else came. (Journal correspondent Robert Keatley, who has visited China twice in the past 15 months.) So you get special consideration because you are from Wall Street."

—"Let's get down to serious business," suggested one editor. Replied the premier: "Why get serious?"

—At the conclusion of the meeting, Mr. Chou said, "I made more replies to your questions than I did to President Nixon, Mr. Rogers and Dr. Kissinger. Dr. Kissinger can talk to you for half an hour and not give you one substantive answer. It would be unfair of me to do that to you. But I understand he has to keep some things confidential."

In a more serious vein, Premier Chou had these other things to say:

FUTURE LEADERSHIP: He gave no hint of the identity of those who might compose a future collective leadership. And he gave no hint when present vacancies in the government might be filled. What the premier stressed was that China had an abundance of middle-aged and younger potential leaders even though they weren't well known to the world.

The world hears only of Chairman Mao, Premier Chou and a few other old leaders at the top and "those who committed mistakes," he said. There are at least 100,000 party officials who have been in the party more than 30 years, he added. "And you can place any among them in a position of leadership and he'll get the job done." People shouldn't worry about future leadership in China, he said. "Those who can do the leading work really are quite numerous."

Because of ousters during the Cultural Revolution and the Lin Piao affair and natural deaths, foreign diplomats here figure the 21-member Politburo has been reduced to 10, five of them army men. Similar gaps have existed for more than a year in the party central committee and in key government ministries, where the post of defense minister is among several long vacant. The diplomats here believe this is because the nation's major power blocs—the party and government bureaucracies, the army and regional leaders—haven't yet resolved how much clout each is to have in the rebuilt government.

RELATIONS WITH THE U.S.: "Some people say developments (since the China visit by President Nixon was decided upon) have been rather slow, but as I see it this isn't so," he said. He mentioned China's entry into the United Nations and the expulsion of the Nationalist Chinese regime from that body as well as the establishment of diplomatic relations with Peking by more than 20 additional countries since that time. Japan was the latest nation to establish ties with China, and it will be followed later this month by West Germany. Each move increases the diplomatic isolation of Taiwan.

"We should look at all these major changes as links in a chain," the premier said. "As I see it, there will be further developments. They may go sometimes faster, sometimes slower."

Premier Chou recalled that when the international table tennis tournament was under way in Japan early in 1971, several members of the United States team applied as individuals to visit China. Chairman Mao had decided the year before or earlier that the time was ripe to improve relations with the U.S., the premier said. But the party central committee and Mr. Chou, according to his version, decided against letting in the Ping-Pong players because they hadn't applied as a team, as the teams of four other nations had.

"Look, a majority of the team wants to come, the time is right and we should take the initiative," the premier quotes Mr. Mao as saying. So on the last day of the tournament the historic invitation was extended to the team as a whole.

"President Nixon, on the occasion of his daughter's marriage, made a joke," Premier Chou continued. "He said if he was unable to come to China, maybe his daughter could. So both sides understood the other. And Dr. Kissinger came to China."

While Dr. Kissinger was here, both he and Mr. Chou were surprised by the victory in the United Nations for the Albanian resolution to expel the Nationalist Chinese regime, the premier said. "It was beyond our expectations," he said.

CHINA'S ECONOMY: Premier Chou reviewed China's current policy of giving first priority to agriculture, then light industry and, third, to heavy industry. And he said he didn't favor replacing Peking's 1.7 million bicycles with automobiles, even when that's possible.

"Peking would become like New York in terms of pollution, and you wouldn't be able to move on the streets," he said.

THE RUSSIANS: He reviewed the history of the Sino-Soviet split and the two nations' border dispute, and he said the U.S. and Japan have much better intelligence on Chinese leadership questions than the Soviets have, "despite the fact they have the largest embassy in Peking, at the highest cost."

He also recalled with relish telling Soviet Premier Alexei Kosygin in 1965: "Now that you don't want Khrushchev anymore, suppose we invite him to lecture

at Peking University about how he developed this crea-
tive Marxism" that Mr. Kosygin had credited him with
on an earlier occasion. But the Soviet premier wouldn't
agree, he said.

TAIWAN: Premier Chou said Taiwan's budget of
about $800 million a year would be borne by the main-
land if it reabsorbed the island. "This would enable the
people there to further improve their lives," he added.
The social systems wouldn't be made the same immediately but would be integrated step by step, he said.

He cited China's treatment of what it calls its "national capitalists" as providing a pattern for Taiwanese
economic integration with the mainland. In the first
seven years after the 1949 revolution, these businessmen were kept in business. In 1956, their private enterprises were absorbed by the state and they were given
interest on their capital of 5% for 10 years, he said.

"Add this to what they made during the years of
private ownership, and it can be said they got their investment back," he contended. "Some are still drawing
salaries as employes of the enterprises. As for Taiwan,
there may be additional steps."

Plunge From the Pinnacle

PREMIER Chou En-lai divulged details of the Chinese government's version of the downfall and death of Lin Piao, who was Mao Tse-tung's designated successor until September of 1971.

The Chinese had said earlier merely that Lin Piao was killed in a plane crash while trying to flee the country after an unsuccessful plot to assassinate Communist Party Chairman Mao and seize power. The now-detailed tale of mystery and intrigue rivals adventure fiction. Even with the freshly added details, there are some among the foreign diplomats stationed here who believe it still may be just that—fiction.

Here is the official Chinese government version as told by Premier Chou:

Lin Piao launched his conspiracy because "he didn't believe that he could really succeed to the leadership," the premier said. "Last year when we criticized within the party the erroneous thinking and political line by Lin Piao, he felt he could not stay on any longer."

Why had Lin Piao's position become insecure? The premier didn't say, but foreign specialists here and outside China believe they have the explanation. The 1966-1969 Cultural Revolution had left the Communist Party and civilian government structures in disarray, following Red Guard attacks on them for elitist attitudes that caused them to lose touch with the people. The Chinese army under Lin Piao, who was defense minister, had been called in to restore order and keep the country running and had assumed enormous power in China's political, economic and social institutions.

When Premier Chou began to rebuild the party and the government bureaucracy, there undoubtedly was a struggle over how much authority over civilian institutions would remain in the hands of the army and how much would revert to party authorities. Chairman Mao threw his support to the premier, and Lin Piao's future started to become cloudy. Foreign students of the Chinese scene also believe that Lin Piao opposed the decision to seek improved relations with the U.S. As early as April 1969, Premier Chou said, Lin Piao read a report to the Ninth National Party Congress that was published in his name but that actually had been prepared by the party's Central Committee. "He only read it out, but his thinking ran counter to the report," the premier said. The report was entitled "United to Win Still Greater Victories." The party Central Committee had earlier rejected a draft that Lin Piao had had prepared for him by Chen Po-ta, a former secretary of Mr. Mao and a Politburo member who was a militant leader of the Cultural Revolution and has since disappeared amid denunciations.

Seeing his path to the succession endangered, Lin Piao began plotting with "a small handful of sworn conspirators" to assassinate Mr. Mao and try to seize power, according to Premier Chou. No attempt was actually made on the party chairman's life, however. "He didn't dare to put his plot into practice because it was only the scheme of a very small handful of people," Mr. Chou continued. "It was only after Lin Piao fled that we got hold of material concerning his conspiracy."

In September of 1971 Lin Piao became "afraid that his designs had been exposed" and prepared to flee on short notice, the premier said. Although Lin Piao as defense minister had the authority to order a plane for his own use, he instead had his son, Lin Li-kuo, deputy head of the air force's operations department, arrange to have a British-made Trident aircraft secretly sent to him at Peitaiho, a seaside resort to the east of Peking.

"As soon as he secretly ordered an airplane, the move was reported because it was not in accordance with our country's normal procedures," the premier said.

When officials asked Lin Piao's wife, Yeh Chun, whether a plane had been ordered, she denied it, and this "showed he was up to something. But at that time we were not sure how big the scheme was," so all airplanes in the country were ordered grounded, the premier said. He continued: "In these circumstances, as he had a guilty conscience, he thought his plot had been exposed, so he fled in great haste by the plane moved there secretly, fearing that he might be caught if he fled too late. Actually, we did not at all think of arresting him, we only wished to know what he wanted that plane for."

The plane took off on the night of Sept. 12, 1971, with a few conspirators but without even the navigator or radio operator, who had become aware of the order that no planes were to take off. The plane headed for Outer Mongolia, where Soviet influence is strong. But "when the plane got there, it failed to spot the runway of the airport and its fuel was nearly exhausted, so it had to try a forced landing." It caught fire in the attempt, and all nine persons aboard were burned to death, the premier said.

How can the premier be sure that Lin Piao was among the nine bodies? he was asked.

"Our embassy people were accompanied to the spot by officials from the Mongolian foreign ministry, and they took photos there," he replied. "Although the bodies were burned, they were not completely destroyed, and it was still possible to identify them."

After the order grounding all aircraft, another group of conspirators took off in a helicopter and tried to flee abroad but never reached the border, the premier said. It was forced to land by Chinese aircraft and "after the forced landing, many secret documents were discovered on board, and among them we found evidence of their plot," Premier Chou said.

News of Lin Piao's death and details of his alleged conspiracy have never been published in the Chinese press. In fact, denunciations of his shortcomings have never referred to him by name, but have lumped him in with another leader who fell from grace earlier. "Liu Shao-chi and other swindlers" is the code phrase, with Lin Piao represented by the latter reference.

But the premier said party and government officials were told about the plot, and later ordinary citizens were informed, presumably at meetings of their local farm, factory or neighborhood organizations. "Now the entire Chinese people know about this matter," he said. "All ordinary citizens, and even children, know about it."

Why did Premier Chou decide now to engage in the first public discussion of the Lin Piao affair by any Chinese leader: One can only guess. A possible explanation is that the purge of Lin Piao's suspected followers has been completed, that the Chinese people have been carefully informed and that they have taken the news calmly. In addition, China may now want the world to see that the plot wasn't widespread, that it was coped with easily, that China has nothing to hide and that the matter should cease being a source of conjecture. That would fit in with China's desire to project to the world an image of calmness, stability and respectability.

Some foreign specialists accept the Lin Piao story, others are openly skeptical, while most suspend judgment. The skeptics question whether Lin would have plotted to kill as revered a national figure as Chairman Mao or would have tried to flee to the Russians, whom he had been outspoken in denouncing in the past. They suggest that Lin Piao might have been pulled from his pinnacle of power by Chairman Mao, Premier Chou and other leaders and, when he wouldn't go quietly, done away with. Then, they speculate, a group of his close followers might have tried to flee by air, were pursued over the Mongolian frontier and shot down. All this is pure speculation, of course.

"About this jigsaw puzzle . . . ," began one American editor, addressing Premier Chou after the tale was told.

"What puzzle?" the premier interrupted. "There is no puzzle about it. I have told you everything. It's much clearer than your Warren Report on the assassination of J. F. Kennedy."

"It's a puzzle to us," the editor replied.

Later, after the premier expressed skepticism that Lee Harvey Oswald had been the sole assassin of President Kennedy, J. Edward Murray of the Detroit Free Press, president of the American Society of Newspaper Editors, told him: "You just have a conspiratorial mind."

Sea Slugs, Tea and Me

CROSSING into China from Hong Kong we walk the length of the covered railroad bridge at Shumchun and approach a half dozen People's Liberation Army men collecting passports at the far end.

I hand mine to one of them. "Okay," he says in English.

On the two-hour train trip to Canton, where we are to board a flight for Peking, the villages, bamboo groves, water buffalo, and green rice fields of the eternal China race by outside the window. But most of our attention is fixed inside the car on Soong Wen-hua, 30, our guide and a representative of the new China. He's responding to questions about his life.

His salary is set at group meetings where his coworkers judge him on his ability, attitude to his work, and loyalty to the principles of Chairman Mao's ideology, he says. Does he earn overtime pay when he works late? He laughs. "We in China take pleasure in our work."

Soong spends 10 hours a week participating with his coworkers in political discussions—indoctrination sessions required of students, factory workers, farmers, soldiers, government officials, everyone. Elsewhere, they generally run four to seven hours a week.

He and his wife have a three-year-old son. What are their dreams for him? "I want to make him something useful to the people," says Soong. It's a predictable, programmed response we are to hear dozens of times from others over the next three weeks.

"I don't have a very good background myself," our guide says apologetically. "My father was a shopkeeper —*petit bourgeois.*" Since the 1966-69 Cultural Revolution chances of being admitted to college or advancing in life have become slim for those whose parents weren't workers, peasants, or soldiers.

Soong takes his three-year-old to nursery school every Sunday afternoon and picks him up again the following Saturday afternoon. We are surprised at this live-out arrangement for one so young. It's optional, to help working wives, and roughly a third of the parents with whom we talk in the weeks ahead avail themselves of this option and profess to see nothing unusual or harmful about it.

It's in the nursery schools, whether of the day-care or boarding variety, where a lifetime of political indoctrination begins, with songs such as this one:

> *We're called little Red soldiers,*
> *We listen to Chairman Mao's every word.*
> *We want to be revolutionaries even when we're young,*
> *We want to be workers, peasants, soldiers, when we are grown up.*

Visiting the historical sites in and around Peking, politics is never out of mind. On the way to the Ming Dynasty tombs we pass one of the ubiquitous red billboards with white characters: "Grasp Revolution and Promote Production." Near the tomb we visit are exhibits showing how the people of that day were exploited to create the emperor's wealth and final resting place.

Signs tell us 35,000 men worked on the tomb for eight years, with every family in the country providing an average of six or seven man-days. The emperor's clothes are displayed and contrasted with the clothes and living conditions of the workers who produced his wardrobe. Dioramas and paintings show peasants being forced to sell their daughters for tax money and other oppression by sinister-looking landlords and agents of the emperor.

Outside buses and open trucks bring a steady flow of sight-seers to view the tombs—and get the message.

The Forbidden City, with its palaces of the Ming and Manchu dynasties, also is crowded with visitors, almost all in the standard blue Mao-style tunics and trousers. Some 300,000 a month walk through the grounds. In the lovely royal garden, with its small and delicate red pavilion, there's another big red sign with white characters saying all this culture is the landlords' culture and came out of the sweat of the exploited people.

Will the steady diet of Maoism and Marxism—in the schools, in the factories, in the press, in the theater —keep the young and rising generation sold on their system and fired with revolutionary zeal? Or will the monotony of it all, combined with the new generation's lack of personal experience with the "bad old days" of widespread destitution, hopelessness, and corruption in China, lead to diminished ardor?

One man's opinion: So long as living conditions and educational and job opportunities continue to improve, most Chinese will subscribe to the ideology. If there should be prolonged deterioration in the standard of life, ideology alone won't withstand the pressure for changes. Individual freedom has been so unfamiliar to the Chinese experience that it is not the vital consideration to most Chinese that it would be to Americans.

For the present, life is improving here, and the enormous majority in this nation of 800,000,000 are able to identify their own material self-interest with the Maoism that preaches subordination of the individual's interest and selfless service to the collective society.

Not all signs in the Forbidden City's palaces and grounds deliver the Maoist message. In the small Hall of Union, which was built in 1420 and served at different times as the empress' throne-room and a storage room for imperial seals, there's a small white tablet at the far end bearing two characters *wu wei*. They mean *laissez faire,* and represent one of the political ideals of ancient China, refraining from central government action whenever possible.

I note the reference in a guide book and point out the stone tablet to an interpreter, who had not mentioned it. "Do nothing," he translates with obvious distaste.

Every meal is an adventure—webbed ducks' feet, sea slugs, sharks' fin, snake soup, turtle, fried sparrows, and lotus root, along with excellent chicken, pork, duck, noodle, vegetable and other dishes. It all tastes much better than it sounds. We note grilled ice cream listed as the last course on one menu and are in a state of suspense throughout the meal. It turns out to be baked Alaska.

The Peking Hotel surprises us with apple pie, to which we deftly apply our chopsticks. We also introduce some names of our own for Chinese fare. Mao-tai, the potent sorghum whisky in which the Chinese drink numerous toasts, is quickly dubbed "the eternal flame." We have a little too much one evening. "You glad table," says the waitress.

Premier Chou En-lai receives our group of American editors at 10:30 one night, a week after our arrival, in a reception room of the Great Hall of the People. There is the usual soldier with rifle and fixed bayonet on guard at the entrance to the buildings and a handful of soldiers in the shadows on the sidewalk in front. Otherwise there's no outward sign of security.

The premier shakes hands with each of us as we

enter the room. A photographer records each hand-shake and the pictures are distributed later as souve-nirs. What appears to be a small grandstand is at one end of the room. It's to elevate the rear rows for a group photograph. All very organized.

After the picture-taking we sit in a large circle, sip tea that's been placed on small tables covered with white cloths, and wipe our hands and faces with hot washcloths provided for that purpose. Chinese Panda cigarets, in blue packages with pictures of two pandas on them, also are laid out on the tables. There's no health warning on the packages.

For more than an hour, the premier seems bent on a filibuster. Questions are answered with long, blow-by-blow accounts of the history of the Communist Party of China. Or lengthy recitals of Mao's political philosophy.

The premier suggests a short break, gets up and goes to the men's room, and when he returns the con-versation suddenly turns fruitful. He talks about the abundance of potential leaders he thinks China has for the future and indicates collective leadership rather than a single successor will take over when Mao dies. He speaks of the country's economic policies and his expec-tation of a larger grain crop this year, and he talks of a 1958 Khrushchev proposal for a joint navy with China and of his satisfaction with the way Sino-U.S. relations are developing.

He spends considerable time explaining why former Defense Minister Lin Piao, who was Mao's chosen suc-cessor, allegedly plotted to seize power in 1971 and how failing, was killed in a plane crash while trying to flee the country. His explanation: Lin sensed his policies were being repudiated by the Communist Party's cen-tral committee and figured he would never be allowed to succeed to the top spot if he didn't move quickly to take power. When he was unsuccessful and feared detection, he secretly obtained a plane and fled in such haste that he left without a navigator or radio operator.

The editors still raise questions. The premier says it's all much clearer than the Warren Report on President Kennedy's assassination and expresses his conviction that Lee Harvey Oswald couldn't have acted alone.

At 10 minutes past 2 in the morning, the meeting breaks up. The editors file out bleary-eyed and yawning. Chou En-lai, who is 74, is bouncy and wide awake.

China's leadership changes have been so frequent that the Museum of the Revolution, across Tien An Men Square from the Great Hall of the People, was "temporarily closed" at the time of the Cultural Revolution and has yet to reopen. First Liu Shao-chi, the chief of state, was ousted, then Lin Piao and a number of others in the next tier of their top leadership.

Apparently the personnel and doctrinal shuffling moved faster than Chinese history could be rewritten and the museum's exhibits reconstructed.

At Peking University we are told about the effort to bridge the traditional gulf in China between those who work with their minds and those who work with their hands. The mandarins, the scholar-officials who long ruled China in the name of the emperors, used to grow their fingernails long as a sign of disdain for manual labor.

Today no high-school graduate is considered for admission to college until he has put in two years on a farm or in a factory. While in college he must spend three months of each year doing such physical labor to "reintegrate" himself with the masses and stay in touch with their thinking. After graduation chances are good he will be assigned to a rural area, where over 80 per cent of China's population lives.

I asked if they had heard of the World War I American song, "How You Goin' to Keep 'Em Down on the

Farm, After They've Seen Paree?" American farm youth have been migrating to the cities. Won't China's educated youth, after they've attended universities in cities like Peking and Shanghai, be reluctant to go back to the fields?

Most of the 1,000 to 2,000 Chinese who flee to Hong Kong each month are not so much disillusioned with communism as they are disillusioned with being assigned to farm work rather than professional work in the cities. Might not the two-year and three-month stints on the farms breed distaste for such labor rather than respect for it and eagerness to return?

Replies Li Chia-kuan, a Communist Party official who's now a top administrator at the university: "As the Han scholar Ssu Ma-chien said, 'The worth of some people's lives is weightier than Mount Tai, the worth of others' lives is lighter than a feather.' "

In the city of Sian, capital of Chinese dynasties from the Eleventh Century B.C. to the Tenth Century after Christ, and now the capital of Shensi Province, we are treated to an evening of music at a local theater. A male soloist sings "We Poor People Follow Chairman Mao." A flute soloist plays "Hearts of the Frontier Guards Turn to the Party." High point is a rendition on the two-stringed fiddle of "Up the Mountain Come the Manure Carriers."

Between culture and serious political-economic reporting, we have a chance to work in some shopping. Bob White of Mexico, Mo., and I each purchase hats appropriate to the Siberian frontier. They consist of huge masses of fur. Our colleagues suggest we mate the two hats and produce little fur hats for everyone in the group. Next morning John Hughes of the Christian Science Monitor complains that White's hat kept him awake all night howling.

Egalitarianism is the rule these days in China, unlike Russia where a privileged, urban-based managerial class sits above the ordinary folk. Part of the purpose of the Cultural Revolution was to rid China of such "revisionist" tendencies. Today factory managers live in the same apartment buildings and in the same size and quality of accommodations as their workers, get along without cars for their personal use, and spend a day a week on the production lines to keep their empathy with the workers operative.

But there is nothing egalitarian about the treatment accorded our group of visiting editors. A Russian-built twin-engine Antonov-24 aircraft is put at our disposal for part of our travels around the country; later it is replaced with a British-made four-engine Viscount turbo-prop. At another time we are transported by private train.

It's ironic that after decades of ranting against the special privileges foreign imperialists carved out for themselves in China in the past, the Chinese now are so effusive in their hospitality to their guests that they volunteer very special privileges indeed.

Everywhere we go in Peking, citizens gawk at us. They have seen far fewer foreigners than we had assumed and drop whatever they are doing to stare at our strange faces and even stranger clothes. In cities and towns away from the capital, large crowds follow us down the street and clap in greeting, or rush to the roadside to wave and clap as we drive past.

The warmth of our welcome is unmistakable. Not only officials but ordinary citizens to whom we speak at random express admiration for America and the hope of friendship. Either strong latent feelings of friendship for America survived 20 years of official hostility and propaganda attacks on us, or the regime is remarkably effective in turning its people's feelings on and off as the party line changes.

Why have we and others been invited to visit China? Partly it's to promote mutual understanding and relax relations with the United States, so the Chinese don't have to worry about us militarily while they dig air-raid shelters and worry about the Russians massed across their northern frontier.

Partly it's in the hope of sympathetic reporting that will depict China as stable, rational, and respectable. This is an image that could not only help enhance China's influence in the world but could further reduce opposition to an eventual switch in diplomatic relations from Taiwan to Peking and eventual absorption of Taiwan by the government on the mainland.

The Chinese mobilized to see that we received the best possible presentation of their system and what they are doing—within limits, of course. We visited showplace factories, schools, and communes, as expected. But this was not purely a Potemkin Village tour.

More often than not, the Chinese were candid in answering our skeptical questions. They made no effort to prevent us from talking to students, workers, farmers, and housewives whom we selected at random, or from knocking on doors and visiting homes at random. We saw much of the bad side—the poverty, the pervasive totalitarianism—as well as the good.

Also, it should be noted, foreign citizens of Chinese extraction are being permitted to visit here in increasing numbers; many of them not only know the language but have friends and relatives here with whom they can probe more deeply into the realities of Chinese life today.

All this reflects a confidence that, despite the many frustrations of life here, the vast majority of their citizens are satisfied with their progress to date and widespread distaste for the present system is not to be found. The Chinese people have no basis for comparison with foreign systems, only with what they knew before.

In Shanghai, Tin Shu-chen, a textile worker, her husband, who works at an electric-power station, and their four children live in a single room and share a kitchen and bathroom with another family of five. This is not unusual.

In a farm commune in Linhsien County in Honan Province, Mao Tsai-chin, who hasn't been out of her village of Ta Tsai Yuan in all her 50 years, has four members of her family living at home. The total income that three of them earned from working in the fields last year was 300 yuan ($130) plus their grain needs.

Yet both profess to feel they are well off.

Mrs. Tin has a bicycle, a radio, a clock, and a sewing machine—and these are the ultimate status symbols to which everyone in China seems to aspire these days.

Mrs. Mao has electric light, which wasn't available in the village until 1964, and a new irrigation project is making the fields more productive than previously. "When I was a young girl," she says, "we had many meals of husks. Now life is much better. We have all this corn and wheat." She points to clusters of corn hanging on the wall outside her house to dry in the sun.

Whether future generations will be as easily satisfied is one of the questions for the years to come. One of the impressions a visitor carries away from China is of larger numbers of children in the village streets, children in the city parks, children marching to and from school, children everywhere. Every seven years there are as many babies born in China as the total population of the United States.

How successfully China feeds, employs, and satisfies its sea of humanity—now one-fourth the human race and still growing fast—is a fundamental question for China's future and that of the world.

Aftermath of a Revolution

WHEN angry Red Guards were storming through Peking to destroy artifacts and habits they considered distasteful reminders of China's feudal past, caretakers at the ornate summer palace just outside the capital grew worried about saving its historical treasures.

But they solved one problem rather simply. Working their way down the long covered walkways along K'un Ming Lake on the palace grounds, they carefully whitewashed all paintings based on ancient Chinese tales. When youthful militants came by, they found offensive scenes already obliterated and left the corridor unharmed.

That was back in 1966, and now the whitewash is slowly flaking away. Thus once more, faces of poets and generals, gods and demons, emperors and their ladies peer down as ordinary citizens wander among the many pavilions and pagodas there. Things appear normal again at that gaudy pleasure resort built by China's last dowager empress with funds meant for her navy.

And that seems true for most of China these days. Law and order have returned after the excesses, exaggerated in the West, of Communist Party Chairman Mao Tse-tung's Great Proletarian Cultural Revolution —a mass movement that removed foes of the aging leader's political line. Most Red Guard organizations have been disbanded while those remaining are carefully controlled by school authorities. Political zealots are being weeded out of party and government with some extremists receiving conspicuous punishment; for example, the man who organized attacks on the British embassy in 1967 was publicly tried in June 1971, and was jailed.

"Political stability has returned," says one foreigner with long experience in China. His view is shared by most analysts in Peking and the West. With renewed stability have come changes that transcend simple law and order. The Chinese government has seemingly regained its self-confidence, although many problems remain, and is able to deal with matters at home and abroad in more normal fashion. Political tensions are easing slowly—fewer Mao badges are worn, for example, and many Chinese don't have to march about like soldiers as much as they did recently.

Meantime, both farms and factories are setting production records; somehow capital investment continued all during the Cultural Revolution. Food and basic consumer goods appear to be in abundant supply, with most families well able to afford necessities.

A steady stream of foreign guests—from Rumania's president to Sudan's minister of animal resources—is flowing through China. An influx of Americans, both official and otherwise, has also begun. President Nixon called, and so did assorted newsmen, concert pianists, and various scientists, among others. Even a few ordinary tourists have now seen the Forbidden City, while U.S. businessmen now call at the semi-annual Canton trade fair.

All this adds up to a nation more self-possessed and self-reliant, an image Peking carefully fosters. The cult of Maoism is being diluted, reportedly at the chairman's own orders. And the mainland government is presenting itself as one able to manage home affairs sensibly and also to assume responsibility in the world community.

None of this means that basic policies have changed. China still values control over Taiwan much more than establishing an embassy in Washington, although it wants both. And it remains militantly Communist, although, of course, its policies differ sharply from those of the Soviet Union, which it thinks has betrayed Marxism.

But the way is being prepared for relative moderation in many fields. Of particular interest in Washington is the possibility of more Chinese participation in settling world problems, such as rights to offshore resources. Peking even pressured, at least indirectly and subtly, the North Vietnamese into seeking a negotiated end to the Indochinese war. The slow trend toward moderation is in sharp contrast to the image of China in disarray, torn by internal strife and determined to destroy all foreign governments it didn't like.

That picture, widely believed, was never quite accurate, although much of the fault was Peking's. And it should be stressed that sharp conflicts did occur and that not all differences are resolved. The ideological leaders of Shanghai, China's largest city, sometimes still go their own way and ignore Peking, it is believed.

Nonetheless, much progress has occurred, partly because the Cultural Revolution has proved more successful than many foreign experts once believed possible. Its origins remain mysterious, and diplomats still debate who won and who lost. Precise information is rare in Peking. But it is clear that Chairman Mao became convinced that China was following the Russian road and was creating a large bureaucratic elite more concerned with its own privileges than with implementing one of his most quoted thoughts—"serve the people." The chairman saw Parkinson's Law run rampant, with self-serving officials not only leading China in wrong directions but even holding back its material progress by "irrational rules and regulations."

His longtime associate and then heir apparent, President Liu Shao-chi, was held responsible for "taking the capitalist road." Chairman Mao set out to get Liu and his alleged associates and succeeded, but the conflict was torturous.

It was more than a simple power struggle. Chairman Mao, Premier Chou and their allies have revamped management of state affairs in ways that, despite confusing rhetoric, are often sensible. Much decentralization and abolition of petty controls have taken place within the basic guidelines set in Peking. Thus, local production units have considerable freedom in managing their own affairs, provided that such political impurities as cash bonuses are avoided. The less such units bother the next higher level of government, the happier everyone seems.

An example of industrial decentralization is the Construction Machinery Building Plant in Shanghai, a small factory of homemade equipment and ramshackle buildings that turns out goods for mines and steel mills. It is supposed to produce as much as possible—just as all other Chinese plants are.

But the real quotas are set during mass meetings of the factory's workers and staff, according to Lee Foling, chairman of its revolutionary committee and, in effect, plant manager. Their decisions are sent to a parent Shanghai organization, but Mr. Lee claims that the parent group makes only "minor" adjustments, which can be vetoed if unreasonable.

Precisely how the annual quota is met is largely up to the factory, which can organize procedures as it sees fit—including spending an annual fund of $40,000 for "technical innovations." This usually means building more homemade production equipment or modifying old machines. Buying sophisticated items from other factories is rare, for China can't afford much modernization. One metal-cutting machine at the plant is a pile of slow-moving rocker arms and flywheels that seem magnificently obsolete but apparently work well enough. A line of homemade machines is called "a dragon of ants" because the machines slowly eat away at huge steel castings, which eventually become ore crushers. Theirs is a pace American industry wouldn't tolerate.

In fact, this system probably isn't quite as democratic as Mr. Lee alleges. "Guidance" from above must be injected somewhere. But in general terms it is true that the state plan is more nearly a compilation of what individual units say they can produce than a detailed blueprint decreed from Peking. Although problems are common, this system does seem to avoid some bottlenecks found in Russian-style management, analysts claim.

Some of this efficiency is new. Mr. Lee now has only 35 staff members, 25 fewer than before the Cultural Revolution. Much needless paperwork has been abolished. Likewise, he no longer must refer routine decisions to a higher level for approval but can assume more responsibility at plant level.

Visits to factories and communes in or near seven widely scattered Chinese cities indicate this is the nationwide pattern. Leaders of Shansi Province even say they have eliminated six-sevenths of all senior bureaucratic jobs at the provincial-government level. "Simpler administration" is a major Mao commandment these days.

Whatever the reasons, it is clear that something in China is working these days, for Westerners agree that record farm and factory production was achieved.

American experts say industrial output rose 15% in 1970 while food-grain production reached 242 million U.S. tons—perhaps 10% less than Premier Chou claimed, but a record anyway.

The U.S. Central Intelligence Agency estimates per-capita income at $130 a year, up 15% from the late 1960s. Many Peking diplomats forecast (accurately) new records for 1971 with regular increases in following years, barring new political upheavals. So far they have been right.

Such turmoil isn't expected though it took China's 29 major political regions many months to form new Communist Party committees, once the process resumed after the cultural revolution. The delay reflects long-running disputes which probably continue beneath the surface. Nonetheless, violence has ended and much unity has been won, thanks to some skillful political manipulation.

Nowadays, political hatred is focused against former President Liu, who is seldom mentioned without adding the words "renegade, hidden traitor and scab." He remains a distant, shadowy figure of evil against whom all other Chinese are supposed to unite. Mr. Liu's fate is unknown.

The fate of another wrongdoer is known, however. Former Defense Minister Lin Piao, once named as Chairman Mao's political heir, was killed in September 1971, when his plane crashed in Mongolia as he was fleeing China. According to Premier Chou En-lai, Mr. Lin had been foiled in an attempt to seize power outright, and thus fled. He is no longer mentioned by name in the press though all Chinese know well who is meant when editorials denounce an anonymous political "swindler" who had "illicit relations with a foreign power"—a veiled reference to the Soviet Union.

No disruptive vendettas are being waged against

others these days. Many local officials who followed "wrong" policies are urged to recant and continue their old jobs. In Shansi Province only 0.7% of party members were expelled for errors—hardly a sweeping purge.

"The Cultural Revolution has brought unity and a single political line," one diplomat friendly to Peking contends. "And whenever in history China had a single political line, the nation was strong. When there were two lines, it was weak."

Some internal relaxation is resulting. Many of Chairman Mao's frequent thoughts remain painted on walls, but some are being covered over rather than retouched as their paint fades. Chairman Mao himself has said the cult went too far and must be toned down.

In Shanghai, brighter blouses and even makeup are reappearing amidst the white shirts and baggy trousers that remain standard female (and male) garb. The number of soldiers assigned to factories is decreasing, and the soldiers are concerned more often with political cheerleading than with serving as gruff commanders. And now that Chairman Mao is greeting visitors, being a foreigner in China is again an all-right thing. Crowds are now more curious than hostile when strangers appear.

Helping to ensure relative calm are the slowly rising standards of living. Cotton textiles, cooking oil and grain are still rationed, but the levels seem adequate. Shanghai longshoremen can buy as much as 55 pounds of rice monthly, not counting the rations for their families. Shops seem to have large amounts of cheap fish, meat and vegetables. Chinese cabbage costs about two cents a pound while fish is sold for 14 cents a pound at Peking's Chau Nei Market. The average factory worker takes home about $25 a month and spends only $3 for rent and $6 for food. And most families have at least two wage earners.

One recent visitor to both capitals says that "compared with those in Moscow, food markets in Peking are a shopper's paradise." And compared with some other capitals, the availability and the low cost of basic needs are startling. This situation occurs partly because few luxuries are available and high prices keep demand for them deliberately low. But visitors find that the Chinese seem well-fed, adequately if drably dressed and healthy. No beggars, street dwellers or starving citizens are seen, as in some other nations. The changes are especially striking to visitors who knew China in the 1940s, when civil war and indifferent government made life miserable for most Chinese.

Such praise must be kept in perspective, however. China remains an underdeveloped agrarian nation and will be so for many decades. Because of its population of at least 800 million, living standards will rise slowly, with levels in the countryside noticeably trailing those in the cities. Bicycles are common, but there aren't any private autos; refrigerators and modern stoves aren't sold; China can't divert steel from such pressing needs as making more railroad tracks.

Likewise, there are rigid social controls that Americans would find intolerable. Perhaps many Chinese do, too—but they don't dare say so. No criticism of any government policy is permitted, and the official press mainly repeats political cliches, leaving little space for news.

The 48-hour workweek is standard, and that doesn't include another six or so hours of mandatory collective study of Chairman Mao's works. China, a nation of great cultural heritage, now permits only eight authorized stage productions, each featuring a thin story line and a heavy-handed political one.

Many backsliding officials have been sent to rural areas for "reform through labor." They may never return. And it is assumed that many "counter revolutionaries" are jailed, but the government never discusses such things.

Another problem is finding successors to the present leadership. Peking analysts commonly say that China can survive Chairman Mao's death because his political line will endure. But these analysts wonder how the nation will react to the death of Premier Chou. This sophisticated government chief is the man directly responsible for seeing that the bureaucracy gets things done as well as for setting China on a more moderate course.

No other official has such wide respect, and no likely successor is apparent now. Diplomats worry how China's aging, often inward-looking leaders will find a suitable replacement. What little is known about other top administrators isn't always encouraging.

One veteran observer cautions that "there are sides to this country that aren't so pleasant." But for most Chinese life today is at least bearable, and there has been a great deal of improvement over the past.

Everyone is employed, housed, fed, clothed and provided with almost free medical care. A national welfare system aids families whose incomes fall below minimum levels. Thus, there is a security most Chinese never knew before; mere survival is no longer a tough daily task. Many may be unhappy with some aspects of Maoism—a stranger can't really find out. But most are believed to credit the government with bringing both personal and national dignity after many hard years.

Says one generally skeptical West European currently in Peking: "You have just got to concede that this government has done a fantastic job in many ways."

The Industry of Make-Do

WOOD SHOP workers at the Shenyang locomotive and rolling stock repair factory are proud of a new "technical innovation" they say results from application of Chairman Mao Tse-tung's thought, the official reason for all good things in China these days.

Their innovation is simple: Rather than burn splintered boards as firewood, they laboriously glue the pieces together to make flooring for freight cars. They show off piles of eight-foot boards, each composed of about 50 wood scraps stuck together with resin they make themselves.

"It's not that we are short of wood" insists Chiang Ting-hua, one of the wood shop's "responsible persons" —the vague term often used to describe Chinese officials. "It's that workers now are masters of their country and want to make full use of all waste materials to develop the economy."

But, in fact, China is short of wood—plus steel, power, capital, technicians and all other basic needs of a modern industrial state. All, that is, except raw manpower. That's why the key word in Chinese factories is now "self-reliance," the official guideline for economic growth in a nation that simply can't afford more-wasteful Western ways. Thus, "relying on our own efforts" is the most quoted instruction of Chairman Mao in places like the Shenyang plant.

And so far it's working. American analysts say

China's industrial growth rate in 1971 was 12%. This follows setbacks and stagnation during the Cultural Revolution, the mass political movement that disrupted much normal life in China a few years ago. Premier Chou En-lai has claimed that among other things the nation now produces more than 15 million U.S. tons of chemical fertilizers and 22 million tons of petroleum yearly. These industries barely existed a decade ago. His figures seem high, but it's generally agreed that factory output set overall records in 1971 and will break them in 1972.

"More important, resources exist for developing new industrial areas in the future," says one foreigner in Peking, who says China recently discovered 44 vast new coal deposits it hasn't publicly announced. So far, in fact, most of this vast nation hasn't been properly explored by mining and oil experts. Thus, someday China may evolve into the major industrial power it wants to be, analysts say.

But that era is decades away. Meantime China is following a homemade do-it-yourself approach to industrialization; this method might have useful lessons for such poor lands as India and Egypt. Visits to factories in three widely separated areas of China give an understanding of how Chinese leaders hope that hard work and native ingenuity can overcome many material deficiencies; these are commonsense ideas that Chairman Mao pushes but that he packages in a unique brand of Marxism often confusing to foreigners.

The visits also give an idea of the enduring material difficulties as well as political problems that persist a bit more tenaciously than Peking wants to believe.

"Self-reliance" means many things in the Chinese context. One aspect is getting maximum use from limited raw materials. Another is manufacturing most, often all, necessary production equipment right in the factory rather than turning to regular makers of scarce capital goods. So-called technical innovations are also included. These often refer to adding homemade devices to existing equipment so a little extra output can be achieved. Above all, it means whipping up a kind of revival-meeting spirit combined with stricter control of the work force.

And it excludes depending on foreign suppliers for essential goods. China once depended on the Russians and had its supplies cut off for political reasons. It doesn't want to repeat that experience with any nation.

The Shenyang factory illustrates many of these points. According to the Communist Party theoretical magazine Red Flag, its workers have "persistently carried out in depth a mass movement to increase production and practice economy, advancing the rapid and all-around developments there as models for other Chinese factories to copy." But a visitor also learns some things the magazine didn't mention.

The Japanese made Shenyang an industrial city during their wartime occupation of Manchuria; the city was formerly called Mukden. But the locomotive-repair plant is even older. Founded in 1926, it has grown to accommodate 9,300 workers in a dozen shops. Its main task is overhauling all sorts of railroad equipment, including steam locomotives, which China still manufactures.

Practicing economy means more than gluing together wood scraps. The factory's wood shop also saves sawdust and shavings, which are pressed into firewood. Other workers pull rusty nails from aged lumber to straighten and reuse. Some make plywood sheets from other scraps for sale to the state. They all say these activities are possible because the Cultural Revolution abolished old bureaucratic restrictions. They interrupt each other excitedly as they explain all this to a visitor.

It all adds up to an approach not economically possible in the West. By modern standards Chinese plants are overstaffed and are involved in peripheral tasks. But in China it works. The nation, with its labor surpluses and resource deficiencies, can afford to have low-paid workers rescuing bent nails and broken boards from the scrap heap. They don't have much else to do, substitute materials aren't available, and Western pricing methods just don't apply.

"It all makes no economic sense by our standards," a West European says. "But they have to do it if they want production increases. In many factories, capacity has been expanded beyond the level of raw materials available."

The pattern applies throughout China. At Shenyang's No. 1 machine-tool factory, metal shavings are carefully saved for resmelting. At another plant, workers retrieve waste from a metallurgical furnace. By adding water to it, they produce gas for welding. Some factories now have devices added to smokestacks for filtering out ash, but it is less for pollution control than to get material for making cinder blocks for construction.

At No. 4 northwest cotton-textile mill in Sian, workers rebuilt what they call a "grain-eating tiger"—a machine that used grain to give texture to cotton cloth. After many errors they found a way to reclaim cotton particles blowing around the factory and use them for adding body to the cloth. They claim the thick homemade goo they now use saves the state more than one million tons of grain yearly.

Another officially encouraged practice is to have factories make most of their own production equipment rather than rely on China's small capital-goods industry. One result is a collection of homemade machines, which sometimes seem inspired by Rube Goldberg. At the Shenyang machine-tool plant, one worker proudly poses by two small presses he has modified. He added a maze of control arms and other devices so the presses stamp metal automatically rather than having to be returned by hand. It looks a bit ridiculous, but it works.

And at the same city's Feb. 13 electrical-equipment plant, named after the date of the 1958 visit by Chairman Mao, Chang Te-ch'un engages in a little self-criticism for visitors' benefit. As chairman of the plant's governing committee, he bought a costly Swiss machine that winds copper wire for electrical components. But the machine works slowly, snaps the wire frequently and makes too much noise. Buying it was a big mistake, he says. This error caused his disgusted work staff to turn to the little red books of Chairman Mao's thoughts and vow to remedy the situation, he says.

Obviously copying key parts of the imported model, they have made simpler machines, which are supposed to work better and more cheaply. Regular production must have suffered during this process, but it seems to be an acceptable price for expanding capacity in a nation short of most manufactured items.

Mr. Chang, of course, gives it all the right political twist, "This was a great education for the plant leadership," says this official, who claims he held erroneous ideas until the chairman's Cultural Revolution enlightened him. "We learned that the working people have boundless ability," he says.

Devising new machines doesn't mean that old ones are discarded. This is a luxury that China can't afford. Elsewhere in Mr. Chang's factory Japanese machines designed in the 1930s are still used to make plastic covers for electrical switches. At each machine, a worker must measure chemicals, insert them into a mold, operate the press by hand and then remove the new plastic case. Ten per hour is the production rate, but China figures 10 of anything is better than none.

In the rush to increase output, China is cutting some corners—perhaps dangerously so at times. For one thing, safety precautions are almost nonexistent in most plants. Lathe operators seldom have eye goggles as protection against flying metal scraps. In an Anshan steel rolling mill, huge sparks fly around the plant as visitors are shown through; a redhot particle lands in one guide's hair, but he brushes it off casually. At a brand-new fertilizer factory near Yenan in Northwest China, insulation is already peeling off pipes that carry noxious gases. The heavy smell of ammonia permeates nearby dormitories for workers in what must be a health hazard.

But the system keeps going, partly because of political policies that skillfully combine the carrot and the stick. Workers now have more say about what goes on in their factories than before the upheavals of recent years. Mass meetings are frequent, and workers are asked to make suggestions or criticisms or pass judgment on production plans. The tactic encourages useful ideas and a broader sense of employe participation, both helpful to efficient management.

In addition, the senior staff must spend some time at manual labor. At the locomotive plant, the office staff was reduced from 1,650 to only 540 after the Cultural Revolution, and one-third of the remaining staff are in the workshops at all times. It is rather like having the president of General Motors tightening door handles four months a year so he will know what it is like on the assembly line.

Bonuses were abolished during the Cultural Revolution, but many workers got pay raises as a result. For instance, on the Shanghai waterfront, when the bonus fund was abolished and divided equally among the workers, it meant another $2.58 a month for each. Meantime, supplies of food and consumer goods have increased, and workers can measure this change by cheaper bicycles, more vegetables and convenient medical services, now usually free. These and similar examples convince many that things are getting better, and they don't want to upset the process.

Not that they could do much if they tried, for the stick is held in reserve. Army men hold key positions at most big factories, mainly to keep political activity along true Maoist lines—such as combating any outbursts of "spontaneous tendency toward capitalism." They rely more on persuasion than on coercion, but state force is available if needed. For example, when labor unions tried to lobby for higher benefits, they were abolished. Many plants have army propaganda teams, which help organize the daily hour or so devoted to mandatory group study of Chairman Mao's works.

At Shenyang's locomotive plant, workers must study Mao for 90 minutes daily, for this plant clearly had extra troubles during recent years. "There were material incentives to poison the ideology of workers," says Hseih Ma-hsia, vice chairman of the plant's revolutionary committee (senior management group) and the only one of three former plant directors who survived the political turmoil.

Rather reluctantly he tells a questioner that workers were divided into three quarreling factions. A key issue was whether to abolish 100 cash bonuses previously available. Finally more than 20 members of the People's Liberation Army arrived and restored order. They organized a mass meeting and convinced workers that the new policies reflected the chairman's wishes—something few Chinese will disobey.

Some army men are still around, although their numbers have decreased, as is true throughout Chinese industry. In fact, one PLA man serves as both Communist Party secretary and Revolutionary Committee chairman, the two top posts at any plant. His predecessors were apparently demoted as "revisionists." Mr. Chang of the plant's governing committee is asked if some workers are happy now to be making less money. His hurt reply: "They don't need more money because prices are stable."

Although Peking talks about "new high tides" in production, this shouldn't be confused with the disastrous "Great Leap Forward" of past years, the pell-mell rush to industrialization that proved so wasteful. Production decisions are usually made at the local level after much mass discussion, a process that seems to weed out bureaucratic stupidities. And although the 48-hour workweek is standard and holidays are few, overstaffing means considerable standing around in Chinese factories. The work pace usually isn't frenzied.

And as rising production figures indicate, tensions in most plants have eased greatly. Despite tales of mass purges during the Cultural Revolution, most managers have survived in senior positions, possibly with titles changed. China doesn't have enough senior administrators and technicians to permit any large-scale firings.

How long progress will continue and tranquility reign is anyone's guess. "How can you motivate everyone to work hard forever without more economic incentives?" asks one U.S. analyst of mainland economic affairs.

But a foreign diplomat based in Peking says the system seems to work better than most outsiders realize. "Many people really are newly inspired to work for the Revolution," he says. "At least enough seem to believe in it to make it last for a long time indeed."

Commune Living—
Chinese Style

THE Aug. 1 People's Commune hadn't been a shining example of Maoist farm policies.

Ignoring Peking commands, many of its 4,000 families slowly expanded their small private plots into the collective rice paddies, often doubling or tripling the size of the family plots. Some of the workers abandoned commune chores entirely, preferring to raise pigs privately, peddle homegrown vegetables in the free market and otherwise pursue what is denounced as "speculation."

"They no longer took part in collective agriculture but in side occupations," complains San Kwang-ta the tough-looking Communist Party official sent out from the nearby city of Shenyang in northeast China to set things right. "Under this practice, the commune's economy was damaged to some extent," he says.

But no more. With help from a political propaganda unit of the People's Liberation Army (PLA), boundary markers separating the private and collective land have been returned to their legal places, free markets been restricted and peasants have been sent back to the rice paddies for communal grain growing. In 1970, this 8,200-acre farm sold 12,000 tons of rice to the state after providing for its own considerable needs. The

1971 goal was for another 3% increase from the previous year's record crop.

"We are teaching the peasants how to implement Chairman Mao's directives for agriculture," the senior PLA man on duty there says proudly.

If visits to six communes in widely separated parts of China are any guide, the ideological backsliding at the Aug. 1 People's Commune was a bit extreme. Nonetheless, similar, if milder, transgressions have occurred but they are being firmly halted these days throughout China.

Renewed emphasis is being placed on the collective side of farmwork. This is a major result of the Cultural Revolution, which sought to stamp out economic individualism wherever it appeared—a practice that the state denounces as "sugar-coated bullets" aimed at killing communism.

The campaign is apparently succeeding. In 1970, American analysts figured that China set a grain-production record of well over 220 million U.S. tons; now many feel Premier Chou En-lai was closer to the mark than they first believed when he claimed output was actually 264 million. Many old China hands find food more abundant than ever before. Meat, fish, and vegetables all are sold without the frantic queuing often found in the Soviet Union, where planners never have solved basic agricultural problems.

One reason is that Peking practices more rural moderation than a scanning of the official press would indicate. Although private plots again are strictly controlled, their continued existence is guaranteed. While most farm households have loudspeakers installed so peasants won't miss their daily dose of Maoist propaganda, these speakers have on-off switches. Strict equality isn't the rule. Those who produce more get paid more.

In general, the forced march to agricultural prosperity has frequent rest stops along the way. The noontime nap is an institution sanctioned by the party.

Because of population density, land fertility and other obvious factors, living standards vary greatly at China's 70,000 communes. But the ground rules under which they operate are uniform.

At least 80% of the nation's 800 million people live in the countryside. Whether China becomes a responsible member of the world community depends largely upon how successful these rural residents are in feeding the 25% of mankind that inhabits the nation. Many foreigners believe Peking's present move toward relative moderation abroad reflects the belief that the farms are doing rather well.

One good place to test that belief is the Red Star People's Commune just outside Peking. It is bigger and richer than most, but it isn't a phony showcase. Like all the other communes, it must earn its own way without much state subsidy. Central-government funds are reserved for key industries, such as those producing fertilizer, trucks and armaments.

The Red Star Commune has 75,000 people living off its 27,000 acres. These people are divided into nine production brigades and 120 production teams (each roughly equal to a village) for easier management. The commune's farm products are diverse: rice, wheat, fruit, vegetables and Peking ducks, among others. The commune also has nine small factories, encouraged by the state, that make mechanical rice planters for commune use, process powdered milk and manufacture rice paper, bricks and grain sacks.

The goal is to make each commune nearly self-sufficient—growing or making most of its needs and earning hard cash to buy those that must come from the state.

According to Shing Chu-wa, vice chairman of its revolutionary committee, or management group, the total value of Red Star's production in 1970 was $21.4 million, up 31% from 1969. The 1971 plan calls for a more modest 8% increase; "we don't make plans so high that we can't fulfill them," he says. About 50,000 tons of grain accounted for most of the commune's income; the 1971 forecast was for 55,000 tons. Mr. Shing knows the party line well and attributed the commune's increases to improved peasant "political consciousness." But a look around Red Star shows that new ditches, more fertilizer and just plain hard work are more tangible factors.

Of Red Star's total income in 1970, the state took about $1.2 million in taxes; the rate apparently never exceeds 6%, and personal income taxes don't exist in China. More than $3 million of goods went into commune reserves against possible bad future harvests, while $5 million worth was divided among the workers. This meant that nearly 60% of income went for seed and fodder or was sold to finance fertilizer, machinery and other needs.

But if the Huang Pao-tsai family is representative, peasants live fairly well. The family has nine members living in a typical village house, which they own. It has a tile roof and a packed-dirt floor. Four members work, giving the family a monthly income equal to about $64. Each adult is allowed to buy 550 pounds of grain yearly from the commune for about four cents a pound. A few years ago the ration was 470 pounds.

A nearby commune shop supplies other needs— lean pork at 36 cents a pound, eggs at about three cents each and vegetables for a few pennies a pound. But like other families, the Huangs have a private plot, where they grow potatoes, corn and beans. And they have a pigpen. Most families raise at least two pigs annually;

they buy piglets from the commune and trade them back later for cash and fresh pork. A valued byproduct is manure, used on the private plot. "Every pig is a little fertilizer factory," explains a peasant at another commune.

Other living costs are low. The Huangs don't pay rent or property taxes. Electricity for their four lights costs about 40 cents a month. Each family member pays 43 cents annually for health insurance; no other charges are made for treatment and medicines, a system installed in the late 1960s.

Bark and corn stalks for fuel cost $2.15 monthly. A smiling grandmother minds the baby when its parents are at work. The government now encourages such family togetherness after a brief fling at a more Marxist way of living in the late 1950s. Families without elder members to act as free baby-sitters can deposit their young at low-cost day nurseries.

The Huang family boasts the standard symbols of peasant affluence: a radio, a wall mirror decorated with goldfish decals, wooden chests for clothes and three bicycles. Because one son is in the army, family members have been sent many Mao posters and busts, which they dutifully display. But they aren't political zealots. During the Cultural Revolution, Mr. Huang says, "I just stayed at my work," as did most Chinese farmers. The turmoil of the cities didn't affect much of the countryside.

The Red Star Commune has resources not found everywhere. It owns 32 trucks, 1,000 horse carts and 120 tractors. More typical may be Horse Bridge Commune near Shanghai, which has only six small three-wheeled trucks, no horses or carts, and 25 tractors.

According to Mrs. Ong Ping-fong, a vice chairman of its revolutionary committee, the Horse Bridge Commune's 36,000 people have only 8,000 acres of land; population density in that area is much greater. Income is still rather low, although new irrigation equipment has been installed and the commune's workshops make concrete sampans, electrical transformers and other goods for cash sale. In 1970, total output was valued at about $3 million, of which state taxes took 5%. The commune's two rice harvests and one wheat harvest totaled 21,500 tons, of which 6,600 were sold to the state, 2,200 went into reserves and more than 3,000 were set aside for seed and fodder. Another allotment went for commune welfare, such as schools and clinics, and for investment needs. This left about 7,200 tons for consumption.

Field workers averaged $163 annual pay, and the average person was able to buy 390 pounds of grain. Both figures were much lower than at Red Star. Even so, Mrs. Ong claims this income figure was double that of 1958.

Thus, no great prosperity prevails in the countryside, but for most peasants there is a security they didn't know before. Every year most communes seem to add a few waterpumps, a tractor or two, or some other evidence of economic progress. Primary education seems universal while most communes also offer some secondary education. In recent years there has been increased emphasis on rural medicine, including "barefoot doctors" (peasants with rudimentary training) and acupuncture specialists (who attempt to cure diseases or relieve pain by inserting needles into key points of the body). Such increased emphasis has improved health standards.

Even so, many obviously aren't happy about existing ways. About 50 peasants daily risk their lives by swimming to Hong Kong, for example. Most of these, however, are disenchanted city youths, often former Red Guards, who were ordered into the countryside as the Cultural Revolution ended. And throughout the land in recent years many peasants took every opportunity to drift toward free enterprise, a grievous sin in Maoist eyes. Especially denounced by Peking are "the Four Freedoms" for which former President Liu Shaochi is blamed. These refer to profit-seeking activities, such as those at the Aug. 1 Commune.

One commune official frankly observes, "Chinese peasants had private land ownership for thousands of years and can't be expected to abandon old habits quickly."

That's why army propaganda teams were dispatched to many communes as policy lines were tightened during the Cultural Revolution. Their numbers have diminished recently, but soldiers still hold many key positions. Four of the nine members of Red Star's standing committee are army men while the Aug. 1 Commune has a dozen soldiers on hand, although none is a member of its revolutionary committee. The soldiers' main task is generally political instruction, leaving management in the hands of veteran commune officials. Mr. San, the party official sent to take charge of the Aug. 1 Commune, is an exception; most other communes are still run, under tighter policies, by the same leaders who were in charge before the Cultural Revolution, frequent travelers say.

This still leaves considerable flexibility at the local level, right down to the production team. At Red Star, Vice Chairman Shing says his committee drafts an annual production plan and then has lengthy discussions with leaders of the nine production brigades, who in turn consult the teams. They try to set realistic goals, but some overriding instructions do come from above. For example, because rice yields per acre are high, all flat irrigated land must be devoted to rice, although communes aren't supposed to waste time growing it where the economics are less promising.

Providing vegetables for nearby Peking is another state goal, but there is some leeway. "If we decide some crop isn't suitable here, we can drop it," Mr. Shing explains. One Westerner declares, "This is the kind of wise government the Russians never have managed to implement."

Once completed, the plan is sent to county leaders for approval. Red Star is located in Big Flourishing County, which includes 15 other communes. Because two Red Star representatives sit on the county's ruling body, there seem to be few serious problems. The Maoist credo discourages outsiders from meddling with local production decisions, provided broad policy lines are obeyed.

Back in the rice paddies, production teams are what most concern the peasants' daily lives. Each team controls a fixed land area—usually what the villagers owned before collectivization—or some other activity, such as dairy barns or machine shops. The workers don't collect regular wages; instead, the teams have a complex point system for determining incomes. Generally, a full day of hard labor is worth 10 work-points, with less demanding jobs graded accordingly. Team meetings are held annually to determine how many points each man deserves per day; the harder a peasant works, the more points he is awarded.

Once harvests are in and a team's collective income is tallied, proceeds are divided according to points earned. This means bumper crops bring bigger individual payouts, a kind of material incentive in a nation that officially rejects such incentives. Members of one Red Star team, for example, earned $215 each in 1970, exceptionally high. A recent visit found its members transplanting rice seedlings, their working area marked by a red flag with Chairman Mao's picture on it.

"Our high pay is due to our political attitude and skill," says a team leader.

China has enjoyed nine consecutive years of favorable weather and seems well into its 10th. Thus, grain imports this year have been cut sharply, an improvement that Americans believe has freed 100 million for other imports.

Perhaps more important, though, are vast changes in the Chinese countryside after the Communists took over in 1949. Ever since, peasants have been hacking away at their farmlands, digging ditches, sinking wells, leveling bumpy fields and otherwise improving the land. There are some dramatic big projects, but the real impact comes from 22 years of steady work at small local ones, regularly improved and expanded. For example, Mrs. Ong of Horse Bridge Commune says underground waterpipes now mean her commune can endure 100 days of either drought or torrential rains without any major effect on crops.

In addition, conservative peasantry has been persuaded to accept new farming techniques. Better seeds, improved irrigation methods, double-cropping and better tools have been adopted. And above all, China's vast rural population is substituting human energy for machines the nation can't yet afford. Everywhere a visitor goes he sees large fields—rather like those of big U.S. farms—with scores of workers chopping weeds, spraying insects, planting new crops and otherwise doing tasks machines would do in America. This intensive use of hand labor also permits up to five crops, such as wheat, corn and assorted vegetables, to be grown together. Farm machines would simply uproot some of the secondary crops.

The Peking government believes this approach— big fields with intensive applications of labor—makes more economic sense than dividing the land into tiny individual patches.

"Learning from the People"

STUDENTS at the Yueh Ya Ch'ang middle school just outside Peking receive the usual course of instruction taught throughout China these days: how farm cultivators work, what Chairman Mao thinks about U.S. imperialism and how to denounce Soviet revisionism, among other things.

They also get quite different classes taught by four special instructors on duty there. Included are close-order military drill, throwing (dummy) grenades and hand-to-hand combat. The teachers are well-qualified; they are regular members of the People's Liberation Army (PLA), assigned to spread what one calls "basic knowledge of military affairs" and Maoist ideology.

"We organize students and teachers to study the latest directives of Chairman Mao so they will have the proper political ideas and correct style of work," says Lo Kwei-shi, the senior military man on hand, who moved to this secondary school from his PLA office job in Peking in 1967.

Sending soldiers to help manage schools isn't a novelty in modern China. All through that vast nation of 800 million persons, the PLA has taken over jobs in politics and production that seemingly would belong in civilian hands.

By some accounts, the Maoist army even gained control of the Communist Party and government, making China more nearly a military dictatorship than a proletarian one.

"The PLA has combined military affairs with study, agriculture, industry, and mass work," the Peking People's Daily boasted in 1971. "The whole nation is learning from the PLA."

But like most generalizations about China, later events proved that talk of a military take-over needed to be heavily qualified. Though army men remain power brokers throughout the nation, the party is once again asserting itself as the major force. "Learn from the people," the army is now told in an effort to teach it humility and restore it to a lesser political role. Yet it still seems true that Chairman Mao's "great proletarian Cultural Revolution"—his mass movement to purge party and government of stodgy, self-serving bureaucrats and reshape the ideology of the common man—has added power to the army in all fields.

Former Defense Minister Lin Piao, once the chosen political heir, is now a deceased foe but the army is still conspicuous at the top. One of Premier Chou En-lai's chief associates is Marshall Yeh Chien-ying, a politburo member who has replaced Lin as Defense Minister in fact if not yet in title; he also plays a key foreign policy role. Military men also have other top central government posts as well as holding senior provincial jobs. And all through China, the so-called revolutionary committees, or management groups, generally include PLA men—whether at the provincial government level or at local factories and communes.

"The present power structure reflects those who had to be brought in to restore order during the Cultural Revolution," an American analyst has explained. "This means the army, plus some holdover bureaucrats." Even though more party men and technicians are being restored to power, the army remains an essential part of the decision-making process years after the Cultural Revolution.

The change in the power structure arose partly from necessity. Chairman Mao no longer trusted party and government bureaucrats to build his type of communism; he thought they were turning intellectually flabby. But the change also came because the venerable leader likes the army, whose austere style he modeled in his own image.

Thus, the Chinese army's control shouldn't be confused with that of a banana-republic junta, with greedy generals grasping for the spoils of office. The PLA's assigned function is to "serve the people," not to emulate the looting hordes of years past that swept across China. Don't steal the peasant's grain or molest his women, the chairman taught long ago—ideas revolutionary in China, where soldiers traditionally were considered a low form of life and a menace to all. The Maoist army, therefore, has always had important assignments in political tutelage and economic production; for example, in 1963 PLA-managed farms delivered 550,000 tons of grain to the state.

Since 1967, the army has been ordered to halt unrest resulting from the Cultural Revolution. And as normality returned, with renewed emphasis on farm and factory production, it seemed obvious that placing soldiers in command would ensure economic and political calm. Thousands of China's three million army, navy and air-force personnel have been given assignments in the civilian sector, some in uniform and others not. Everywhere a visitor goes he finds them in management positions, generally as pragmatic substitutes for civilian radicals who brought on most of the turmoil of recent years. (Many veteran administrators and technicians who are more interested in production than extremist politics have retained their posts, however.)

This makes the PLA the elite force of Chinese communism. Every Chinese boy (and girl) learns that army men represent the Maoist ideals of selfless labor and study; "fear neither hardship nor death" in building and defending the nation, the chairman says. And every parent knows that military service gives a youth the best possible start in life; even if he is mustered out after a few years, PLA service looks good on the record.

The entire state propaganda machine praises the army lavishly and thus encourages recruitment. Current posters, for example, honor soldiers who fought the Russians during 1969 border clashes. Yet joining isn't easy. The PLA maintains high standards and can choose from 150 million youths—both male and female—of military-service age. Finding enough volunteers isn't a problem, even though a private's pay is only about $2 a month.

Current guidelines for army work were set forth by Chairman Mao in 1966: "The PLA should be a great school. In this school our army should study politics and military affairs, raise its educational level and also engage in agriculture and side occupations. It can also do mass work, so that the army will be forever at one with the masses." The late Edgar Snow, an American writer who often visited China, put it this way in early 1971: "All China is a great school of Mao Tse-tung thought, and the army is its headmaster."

How cheerfully the masses welcome this tutelage may be questionable. But whether they like it or not, the PLA has moved into command positions everywhere. For example, four of eight senior officials of Shansi Province who in mid-1971 told foreigners about developments there were in uniform. Li Chen-ping, a civilian vice chairman of that province's revolutionary committee, said some foes of Maoism had been in office previously. "The struggle was fierce," he said, "but with the firm help of the PLA we dragged out that handful of renegades and seized back that portion of power taken by them." And gave it to the army, he might have added; PLA members took 29 of the top 110 posts in the province.

What such events mean for China's future is a matter of much speculation. Few of the new commanders are known to the outside world, and their political views remain a mystery. But these army men are rising to power when China is beginning to steer more moderate courses at home and abroad; if they were violently opposed, the experts say, it is unlikely that Ping-Pong diplomacy would have begun or that President Nixon would have been invited to Peking. And given the PLA's historic concern with political calm and economic production, radically new internal policies don't seem likely either.

A month's travel in China can give some ideas about how the army functions in the civilian world and what its commanders seek.

Clearly, basic law and order is one objective. At the Yueh Ya Ch'ang school, chaos reigned before the soldiers arrived—30 strong—in late 1967. Student factions were busily hanging big posters denouncing each other, while Red Guards from elsewhere were camping at the school to exchange "revolutionary experiences." Schoolwork stopped, and many teachers were being criticized for political backsliding.

According to PLA man Lo, the soldiers ended all that. They organized mass meetings and convinced students that Chairman Mao didn't like such turmoil. Force wasn't used, he says, but it seems obvious that it was available if needed. In any case, the students formed a single Red Guard organization, the visitors went home and classes resumed. (Nowadays the Red Guards form a kind of honor society, whose main activity seems to be close-order drill on Saturday afternoons.) Some teachers had to confess to past political errors, but none lost their jobs. Calm returned, and all but four of the soldiers departed.

This desire for order is evident elsewhere. On Shanghai's No. 5 dock, which handles foreign trade, the boss is Niu Jui-hua, a stocky man in work clothes who looks like any other tough longshoreman. But until 1969 he was one of the "cadre" (army ranks were abolished in 1965) in the PLA construction corps; he was sent to the waterfront to end bickering among workers and get cargo moving again. "Members of the cadre often go back and forth between civilian life and the PLA," he explains.

As calm returns, the number of troops on economic duty declines, although many key civilian positions seem to have become permanent PLA property. At the Red Star Commune near Peking, only 30 of the original 100 soldiers remain, but four of the nine top jobs there belong to the army. The factory boss and Communist Party chief at Shenyang locomotive-repair plant is an army man; he has, however, sent back about 20 soldiers who arrived there in 1967 to help end local disputes. "We reduce the numbers as the need decreases," one production official says.

The remaining men are often members of "PLA political-propaganda units," on duty to provide ideological cheerleading. They organize Mao-study meetings, watch for economic backsliding (such as payment of forbidden material incentives to workers) and in general dispense the latest party line. But they often pitch in at the hardest tasks; the PLA is supposed to be not an occupation force but a model for ordinary workers to emulate. Soldiers in the countryside more often are seen carrying shovels than rifles.

But if restoring order is one objective, keeping

power in army hands seems to be another. The new revolutionary committees (for economic management) and Communist Party committees (for political guidance) seem to have army leaders installed at or near the top permanently, not just as caretakers until the old bureaucracies function again.

"PLA leaders are conservative in that they are law-and-order men and also in that they have power and want to keep it," a leading U.S. analyst says. "But their views on other matters, such as foreign policy and allocation of economic resources, remain unknown."

Increased production, however, does seem to be another army goal, and it is being pursued through practical methods rather than utopian "great leaps forward." The army encourages Mao-decreed "self-reliance" at farms and factories and tries to keep workers concerned about what they produce and how they do it. Soldiers may be bosses, but they apparently know their technical limitations. At a hospital in Wuhan, for instance, the army man in charge presided over a recent staff meeting with foreign visitors. But he didn't try to answer technical questions; he shunted them to appropriate experts and didn't kibitz. The visitors came away convinced that he had a friendly working relationship with his staff and didn't play the role of a gruff commander.

Another military duty is teaching the public rudiments of military training, primarily defensive. This is in accord with Chairman Mao's high regard for military science and his belief that discipline and organization are good for the masses.

But the regimen doesn't seem onerous. At the Yueh Ya Ch'ang school, for example, the teen-agers get military drill as part of their twice-weekly physical-education courses, along with Ping-Pong and basketball. During vacation they get another 20 days, but these seem to include more drill and exercise than straight military training. Do they fire rifles? PLA man Lo is asked. "No, of course not," is his slightly shocked reply. "They are too young."

But few are too young for some indoctrination. Children can buy toy rifles, whose bayonets can be jabbed into paper tigers labeled "American imperialism." Even four-year-old girls sing songs about fighting foreign foes. One line goes: "Sha, sha, sha," ("Kill, kill, kill").

Older folks get more serious training as members of the militia, a kind of home guard that includes most able-bodied persons and that was recently made an official part of the PLA. Of the 1,812 members of the Double King production brigade, which works near Sian, 480 have enlisted in the militia. And of these, 270 are in the younger (age 16 to 30) "backbone" section. It seems that few have weapons available, however. And while workers at a clock factory near Anshan get weekly air-defense practice, pointing dummy rifles at moving model airplanes or balloons, they don't fire at anything.

The PLA is an elite force—but one with problems. One is a long-running internal dispute about politics versus military professionalism. Guerrilla warrior Mao has a "millet and rifles" approach to logistics and opposes excessive reliance on modern weaponry. But his commanders sometimes have other thoughts as they peer across the 7,000-mile-long Sino-Soviet-Mongolian border at about 42 first-class Russian divisions arrayed there. In fact, some have been fired for wanting more rockets and fewer Mao-tracts.

Still, armies on both sides of the Sino-Soviet border are being upgraded these days, although more in quality than in quantity. Both the Russians and the Chinese are deploying better combat aircraft, air-defense systems, armor and other modern weaponry. ("This strengthening of forces says something about both sides' attitudes toward their long-term relationship," one American expert says. Many analysts, in fact, believe that the PLA's worries about Soviet intentions help explain the current thaw in Sino-American relations.)

The PLA has 118 well-trained infantry divisions, plus some armor. The Chinese army however, "remains largely an infantry force with serviceable but often outdated equipment," according to the British Institute for Strategic Studies. Despite new arms programs, the experts believe that the PLA will be short on mobility and firepower for many years.

So far, China's military spending has been relatively small; a U.S. government study estimated it at only $7.5 billion in 1968, meaning that China didn't rank among the top 30 nations in dollars spent per man in uniform. But recently there have been hints that military spending is rising. An increase in outlays could lead to serious debates between civilians and soldiers about how to spend China's resources—on fertilizer or jets, for example.

A lesser problem for the army may also be developing. The official press occasionally accuses some PLA cadres of "arrogance" and "complacency" in civilian work. Apparently, in violation of chairman Mao's basic teachings, some army men treat civilians high-handedly and stifle local initiatives. Now and then the press has cited examples: "Even if we want to do something, we don't get a chance," one civilian complained.

In fact, this developing attitude, compounded by the Lin Piao affair, caused Peking to remind the soldiers that they should "learn from the people rather than drift into the high-handed ways that armies of old China followed."

Mao's Words and
Worldly Miracles

THE paddy fields of Horse Bridge Commune just outside Shanghai are lush and green, promising yet another record harvest this year. And the reason is simple, according to commune officials. They encourage the rice with heavy doses of dialectical materialism, as taught by Communist Party Chairman Mao Tse-tung.

"It is because we apply the revolutionary ideology of Chairman Mao in a living way that we obtain high and stable yields," says Mrs. Ong Ping-fong, a vice chairman of the commune's revolutionary committee, or management group.

She is hardly alone in this view. All over China loyal officials credit Chairman Mao's widely assorted thoughts with producing new achievements in grain growing, brain surgery, aircraft maintenance and the collection of human manure (called night soil) for fertilizing the fields. With correct application of the chairman's philosophy, visitors are constantly told that "worldly miracles" will result and that spiritual forces will be transformed into material gains.

Surprisingly enough they are often right, although most Westerners have trouble understanding the connection between bumper harvests and the Little Red Book of Chairman Mao's. His thoughts that affect most Chinese most often incorporate large rations of common sense and simple science, packaged in Communist jargon.

At the Horse Bridge Commune in east China, Mrs. Ong says that application of what she calls Mao-think would be good for rice farmers everywhere. "The peasants used to believe that the more water on the rice, the better, so they flooded the fields whenever possible," she explains. "But then they were taught that rice grows in three distinct phases, each requiring different irrigation methods. Thus, nowadays they control water application more scientifically, and bigger harvests result. Once peasants grasped the objective laws of rice in accordance with Chairman Mao's philosophy, they began obtaining high and stable yields."

What all this has to do with Marx and Lenin is sometimes obscure, but it makes sense in the rice paddies, especially in China.

Chinese intellectuals long have scorned both systematic scientific inquiry and manual labor, leaving peasants to plod along in traditional ways without benefit of technological discoveries. Along with other social constraints, this attitude discouraged innovation in farming and most other phases of Chinese life. Historians say the resulting atmosphere of orthodoxy helps explain China's fall from greatness in recent centuries; the nation became a helpless giant. The pattern led to political revolution and communism.

Chairman Mao is out to abolish all remnants of this orthodoxy. Chinese intellectuals no longer let their fingernails grow long to prove they are above working with their hands; they are ordered into the countryside, at least briefly, to learn what rural China is all about. Workers are told not to accept factory bosses' instructions meekly but to complain when they think things are managed badly.

At all levels, both office and manual workers are

encouraged to figure out their own problems and deal with them locally rather than rely on higher officials to rush to the rescue. Scientific investigations, technological innovation, self-reliance and just plain hard work form essential parts of the chairman's teachings—concepts that some analysts note wryly should be dear to any capitalist heart.

And many China specialists agree that such concepts, rather commonplace in the West, are desperately needed if China is ever to achieve relative prosperity for its 800 million people. They say these ideas would have to be encouraged no matter who ran the country. The old system obviously broke down and was no longer able to provide basic needs for the nation's huge population. Whether such concepts need be packaged in Marxist jargon is another question, although a somewhat hypothetical one. Chairman Mao clearly believes so, and he is in charge.

Thus, in northeast China, at the Red Flag Chemical Fertilizer Factory near Yenan, the local party secretary, Wang Tien, says the new plant was able to begin production on time in 1970, thanks to the chairman's teachings. They helped an inexperienced staff overcome lack of technical training and encouraged members to try harder rather than give up.

For one thing, after political study, they solved a transportation problem by modifying four-ton trucks to carry eight-ton loads, he says.

In central China, at the Double King Production Brigade, part of a commune near Sian, peasants sing about the chairman's "eight-point charter for agriculture," which they call a great ideological victory in farming. The eight points, however, call for such mundane practices as deeper plowing, closer planting and better seed selection.

Not all the chairman's instructions are like advice

from a county agent in America's Midwest. The Chinese people also receive large doses of his other thoughts, which include advocacy of world revolution, fighting "American imperialism" and crushing any internal opposition to the Maoist line. Peking uses this ideology to pursue many objectives that Washington considers rather nasty. It arms guerrilla movements in various parts of the world, tests nuclear weapons in the atmosphere and tries to undermine Western influence in many areas. But Chairman Mao's thoughts are flexible —his new "revolutionary foreign policy" (as it is officially called) permits him to have Richard Nixon to tea, while making clear to Hanoi that proletarian solidarity has its limits.

When Rumanian President Nicolae Ceausescu called on the chairman in mid-1971, Mr. Mao met him with this thought, duly recorded in the Peking press: "Greetings to you, Comrade. May you do even better. Unite and overthrow imperialism and all reactionaries." Thus spoke the chairman even though Rumania tries hard to maintain friendly ties with both "imperialists" (Washington) and "reactionaries" (Moscow).

Throughout China the populace is exhorted to aid "revolutionary peoples" everywhere as they fight imperialism and is reminded that the Soviet government means China no good.

Likewise, the chairman's quotations are used to justify the strict discipline, physical and ideological, that the state imposes. In Maoist country, economic or intellectual deviation hasn't any place. Everything and everyone hews to the Maoist line. For example, one of the few so-called cultured works that sophisticated Chinese are allowed to see is a Peking-style opera called "On the Dock."

This tale of the Shanghai waterfront, with an exceptionally thin plot line, tells how an agent of Chiang

Kai-shek, seeking to discredit Chinese communism, puts glass fiber in a sack of grain bound for Africa. After three long hours the villain is discovered, a young boy is politically remolded and everyone sings in praise of Chairman Mao. In all Europe, probably only Albania would dare stage such a simplistic story with its heavy-handed political sermons.

Yet many of these exhortations seem more form than substance, a kind of mental tax duly paid by citizens for whom the thoughts have little practical meaning. More often, their mandatory study of Chairman Mao's texts focus on things that help break down dependence on higher-ups to solve local problems. "The tendency in China in the past was to wait for wisdom to be handed down from above—but no more," one Westerner based in Peking says.

As Chairman Mao has stated, "On what basis should our policy rest? It should rest on our own strength, and that means regeneration through one's own efforts."

Consider the case of Liu Hsieh-hua, for example. She is a pert 22-year-old in baggy blue trousers and faded pink shirt who works in the Yenan fertilizer factory. On the wall of her crowded dormitory room, shared with four other girls, are notebooks whose large Chinese characters describe her "experiences" in studying the chairman's thoughts (this writing practice is encouraged throughout China). Some accounts are jargon-filled critiques of revisionism, the evil practices allegedly encouraged by deposed President Liu Shao-chi. But others are more to the point.

It seems that the lab in which Miss Liu works had a tough assignment recently; it had to produce a copper compound that some of its young workers had never heard of, let alone manufactured. But they turned to the chairman's pamphlet entitled "On Practice" and began experiments. After chemical analysis and many errors, they finally produced the compound satisfactorily, and work continues smoothly, the girl explains. All this is duly recorded on her wall.

The point is that such attitudes aren't traditional for the Chinese. Although they produced many inventions long before the West—gunpowder, printing, the wheelbarrow and the compass among them—a cohesive program of continued research and development didn't exist. "In short, science failed to develop as a persisting social institution, as a system of theory and practice socially transmitted," Harvard historian John King Fairbank has written. Many of Chairman Mao's writings and the enforced application of them in what Peking calls "a living way" are supposed to change this attitude.

Many think the attempt is working. For example, a European Communist diplomat notes with grudging admiration that peasants at communes now fix their own equipment when something goes wrong. "They don't wait around for the state to send spare parts as they do in my country," he says.

The chairman apparently believes that by including such everyday matters in the study of his overall political theories, he can get tradition-minded Chinese to adopt scientific attitudes toward their work. And presumably he expects the results of his practical advice to convince people that his ideology is correct on all counts.

He also tries to develop social consciousness in a nation that has been family-oriented for many thousands of years. Thus, "serve the people" is a frequent instruction. This is often applied literally; stores must stagger their hours so workers can shop at convenient times.

Overcoming the traditional Chinese aversion to physical labor as demeaning is another Maoist goal. A party worker in Shansi Province named Wang Yueh-shu wrote that he managed to mix with ordinary peasants only after giving up such old-fashioned ideas.

He says he first worked outside a pigsty, leaving the dirty work to veteran farmers because he didn't want to get his clothes dirty. But after thinking about the chairman's instructions, Mr. Wang realized that the pigsty wall was in fact a political barrier separating him from the masses. Plucking up his courage, Mr. Wang leaped over the fence and joined peasants in cleaning out the manure.

Bargaining in Kwangchow

A SHREWD Yankee trader by the name of Julian Sobin has just returned from one of the seemingly endless bargaining sessions he had been holding with equally shrewd Chinese traders.

"God, I've had 30 cups of tea today," he mutters under his breath. "If I have any more I'm going to float into the hotel." Flopping into a straight-backed chair and hunching forward, Mr. Sobin reviews the day: "Everybody shakes hands. It's a big deal to shake hands. Everybody asks about my wife. We talk about the heat in the room. We then review the failure of communications between America and China for 23 years. We have a conversation about mutual benefit. We exchange more amenities. By this time, we've gone through a couple of cups of tea.

"Then, they make very clear when we've stopped the horsing around. The mood and the subject suddenly change, and they say, 'Have you reviewed the subject we discussed yesterday?'" And Mr. Sobin plunges into tedious bargaining for the chemicals he wants to buy.

That's pretty much the routine in Kwangchow at the semiannual, month-long Chinese export commodities fair, the biggest event there is for anyone anxious to trade with China. There is lots of small talk, lots of tea, an occasional chiding over politics and then, all at once, the Chinese get down to business and it is all work. However it goes, it is the Chinese who direct the proceedings, buying or selling, and the Western trader who has little choice but to follow their lead—and, most often, to accept their terms.

The pace is erratic and grueling, and it goes on into the early hours of the morning as weary businessmen huddle over papers in their sparse hotel rooms to prepare themselves for the next day's haggling. At 8:30 sharp—the Chinese pointedly stare at their watches when a businessman is late—the dickering begins anew in the immense, gray stone trade hall on Haiju Square in Kwangchow.

Here, between display cases of microscopes and synthetic diamonds, wedged next to industrial machines and sitting under big red signboards emblazoned with quotations from Chairman Mao, businessmen from about 100 countries sip Jasmine tea, smoke the Peony-brand cigarets invariably pushed upon them and negotiate actively, and often with mounting frustration, with their inscrutable hosts.

"Everybody beats everybody over the head like mad because everybody wants a piece of the cake," says a Dutchman with long experience attending the trade fair. Maybe the cake won't turn out to be so great, he admits, "but we all have expectations, and we want to get on the record—so we buy at ridiculous prices."

An estimated half of China's imports and exports, which came to about $4.5 billion in 1971, is negotiated at the two trade fairs held here every year, or in the days right after the fairs. Even big capital-goods pacts negotiated and signed in Peking, such as Boeing Co.'s 1972 $150 million sale of 10 jet aircraft, originate from contacts made here. "If you do not attend the fair, you do not get the chance to do other business," says a veteran trader.

China has been holding the fair in Kwangchow— known to Westerners as Canton—since 1957. To that first fair came barely 1,200 businessmen; in the spring of 1972, 21,000 attended, and as many as 25,000 were expected to show up at the fall 1972 fair. There are perhaps 80 American traders among those 25,000 this time, up from 40 or so in the spring of '72, and, of course, none at all before that.

Clearly, those 80 Americans are at a disadvantage. But even the most jaded European traders say each fair is an unnerving experience. The Chinese, they say, change the rules each time.

"Years ago, we bargained, but now it is take it or leave it," is the advice a confident Swede gives a novice American on the train into Kwangchow. The next night, he saunters over with new word: "All of a sudden, you can bargain again. I went in and they said, 'Whatever is convenient.' " The day after that, however, the Swedish trader has changed his tune again: "Forget it," he snaps. "We're back where we started."

For their part, the Chinese say they expect trade with the rest of the world to increase "rapidly," while trade with America will "develop step by step." Indeed, words like "gradually" and "step by step" are part of the litany when Chinese, both those highly placed and those not so highly placed, discuss trade with America. The "steps," of course, can be big ones. In the first half of 1972, American corporations bought $16.6 million in Chinese goods, which while small was more than triple the figure for all of 1971. China's purchases from U.S. companies have been even larger, though most of them are one-shot deals like the one with Boeing.

Clearly, the Chinese are more interested in selling to the U.S. than in buying from it—after all, they point out, the main purpose of the fair is to sell. Still, last spring they did give some Americans broad shopping lists of what might interest them, and the Americans this time are back to sell. Mr. Sobin, president of Sobin

Chemicals Inc. of Boston, represents 31 U.S. companies here, including Wyeth Laboratories, which hopes to sell the Chinese birth-control pills. Some of his other clients believe they can sell pesticides, fibers and plastics to the Chinese.

Whatever it buys, China is likely to look at America only for what the Chinese can't find from long-established trading partners. "We have told our clients not to offer anything that can be purchased elsewhere," says Mr. Sobin.

Mostly what America has to offer China, traders here agree, is technology. "They are at the point, we think, where they want to build in the whole technical structure of a modern industrial society," says David C. Buxbaum, president of May Lee Industries Inc., a New York company that specializes in China trade. Mr. Buxbaum envisions China buying computers and their software, more aircraft, communications equipment—China has 250,000 phones in a country of almost 400 million square miles and over 700 million people—mining equipment and pollution-control devices. David Cookson, another American trader, believes the Chinese will also be in the market for American construction equipment—of 300,000 miles of roadway in China, only 1,000 miles are paved—equipment for the oil industry, paper and pulp, agricultural chemicals and synthetic fibers.

Clearly, consumer goods aren't high on the list of goods China hopes to acquire from the U.S. The Chinese aren't much interested in such "frills," and they feel they produce enough consumer goods of their own. Exhibit cases here are filled with homemade cameras and film, TV sets, baby bottles, medicines, razors and even window air-conditioners.

Chinese officials themselves are extremely circumspect about their shopping list. "Maybe you have some products in the technical (field)," says Peng Chin-po, deputy secretary general of the fair. "If we find it necessary, we can place some orders." Coming from the normally tightlipped and noncommittal Chinese, that is a remarkable statement, tantamount to an admission of desire.

But the Chinese, as well as American traders, say serious impediments to trade still stand between the two nations. China invited Americans here and set up a dollar currency exchange to facilitate trade. Now, it is understood, they feel America should reciprocate.

Most galling to the Chinese is the fact that China hasn't gotten most-favored-nation status, which means its goods must pay substantially higher U.S. tariffs than products from other nations. For instance, chemical duties are roughly double normal duties; for knotted carpets the tariff is four times the usual rate. There are also other snags to increased trade, many of them policy hang-overs from the 1960s and 1950s, when the U.S. viewed China as the implacable enemy. Why, the Chinese ask, can they mail parcel post packages to America and the U.S. Postal Service delivers them, but if an American tries to send a package to China, the U.S. post office won't accept it? Still other snags: frozen Chinese assets in America and frozen American assets in China; and various American regulations restricting shipping and long-term credits.

All that irritates American traders as much as, if not more than, it annoys the Chinese. "The ball is in the American court," says Mr. Buxbaum. "American corporations are in serious competition with others, and we can't wait around. There is tremendous opportunity for sales in China. If we let it go by, someone like the Japanese who are very aggressive will take it."

For the most part, the polite Chinese seem to welcome and be fascinated by individual American visitors

—though anyone who tries to cross the bridge from Hong Kong to China with a Taiwan visa in his passport is likely to receive a brief but stern lecture from a People's Army guard to the effect that "There are not two Chinas. There is only one China in the world."

The welcome Americans receive from other Westerners at the fair is less than enthusiastic. "Ah, the bloody enemy," says one European on the Hong Kong-to-Canton train when he hears an American accent. There are mutterings on the same train that the rich and naive Americans will probably bid up prices and be greeted with the kind of red carpet treatment other traders never got from China. (Sure enough, the Hotel Tung Fang here has reserved its most prestigious floor for Americans and has added apple pie and ice cream to its menu.)

One Englishman recalls the bad old days, which American traders, of course, didn't have to go through. "There was indoctrination every night. People would come to your room and read to you from the Red Book incessantly." The Americans, he says, are getting in "without going through the bitterness and the propaganda and the indoctrination."

The city foreigners see here is one of three million people and about as many bicycles. Old women wearing red arm bands direct traffic. Westerners may walk freely about the city and at night often spend much time over long Chinese meals in innumerable fine restaurants. (Old European hands can be spotted easily— they are the ones with the foresight to bring their own liquor and instant coffee.) The Chinese on the streets invariably cluster to stare at the foreigners—though few Western businessmen have gotten such looks as one shapely young German girl who is seen—and seen and seen—around town in a mesh, see-through minidress and high platform heels.

There is nothing like that in China. There is, however, plenty at the trade fair to surprise Westerners who have always thought of China as an industrial infant. Products on display are diverse and often sophisticated. They range from canned lychee nuts to digital computers, electron microscopes and a furnace for growing crystal silicon for electronic parts. (It is impossible to tell immediately which are one-of-a-kind items and which are production units for sale.) Other products seen at the fair: a ship's binnacle, preserved dissected rabbits with each part labeled, surveying gear, goat skins dyed to look like panda, pots and pans, toilets and even some mod clothing.

The Chinese use the fair to show off their drive as well as their products. There are numerous exhibits of how the "broad masses" of the commune or factory have tamed raging waters or returned alkaline soil to productivity or built a hydroelectric station, many of them manned by some of the broad masses who did the work themselves.

Few businessmen take the time to wander through the exhibits, however. Here, the business of the day, every day, is business. Westerners often accuse all Chinese of practicing the same infuriating bargaining tactics, but that obviously isn't so. Even on the first day of the fair here, some buyers could be seen at the cable desk in the fair building shooting home messages reporting purchases of 10,000 units of this or 5,000 tons of that, while others remained at the bargaining tables, mired in details and demands that threatened to drag out for weeks. It is impossible and rather foolish to categorize Chinese business methods. So what follows are impressions and observations of widely scattered negotiations over a few days at the fair.

Most negotiating is done right in the open for all to see, on tables covered with white cloth and topped with glass sheets that fill the halls of the fair building. Traders waiting their turn watch—and sometimes eavesdrop—uncomfortably as their competition huddles with the Chinese. Sometimes the bargaining is so unproductive that many businessmen stay on after the fair in hopes of peddling their goods to what they, one and all, consider the largest untapped market in the world. "You keep going until somebody gives out," says Mr. Cookson, the American trader.

"They play one off the other," says an Englishman who has come to more than 20 fairs. "You sit and talk for two hours, and you are about to give up when they give you just a little bit and say, 'Come back next week.' They can be very tough when they want to buy." A Britisher who deals in chemicals says the Chinese approach can be maddeningly indirect. After much courteous stalling, "they say, 'Your prices are too high.' 'How much?' you ask. 'Too high,' they answer. 'Well, 2% too high?' you ask, and they all laugh. 'Well . . . 5% too high?' and they all laugh again—but not so loudly."

In follow-up communications, the Chinese can be more blunt. One American tells of a letter he received following the fair in early 1972. "This deal has finally been concluded," it read, "although you dragged the negotiations on for quite a long time."

The Chinese expect foreigners to be themselves. An American says he took the advice of two Europeans and tried to be reserved and stiff in his dealings. "It didn't work. So I went in the next day and was my usual brash self—and that did work." On the train coming to Kwangchow, veteran traders routinely snicker at newcomers poring over the Red Book of Chairman Mao's Quotations. Such falsities don't impress the Chinese, they say.

Politics can enter in, however. One American received a lecture on the "hostile act" of American planes in bombing the French consulate in Hanoi. The harangues of past years are gone, however, and now the politics the Chinese discuss is most often U.S. politics.

The Chinese are equally fascinated with foreign marketing and often want to know in great detail how the buyer plans to distribute his purchases and who likely will use them. Because of this, traders say, it is generally unwise for big corporations to send top people here; the Chinese expect a man who not only has the authority to negotiate but also can answer the most precise and detailed queries. "No big corporation president can really be effective here," says one trader.

But while the Chinese exhaustively seek out details, they aren't so eager to part with the kind of detailed information foreign traders want to receive in turn. In the medical hall, one foreigner dickers for half a dozen portable operating tables. Such tables are in short supply, the Chinese respond. "Look, I'll wait a year for delivery," he pleads. The circuitous reply: "Will you come to the next fair?"

Says an Australian: "There is a chemical I want, and they said they didn't have any. When I pressed, they just asked if I'd raise my price from last year by 10%." The same man also ordered another chemical and specified he wanted it in needle form, not in granule form. The Chinese replied they might ship either. He asked for an option in the contract for protection. He was refused. "We will try for needle," he was told. He pressed the issue. "We will try," he was told. The Chinese didn't budge. The Australian did.

Chinese bargainers tend to operate by a set plan, traders say, and they can be thrown off by the unexpected. If a fact enters in that they haven't been aware of, they feel they have lost control and grow timid. Says Mr. Cookson: "All the negotiators are . . . the 'mouthpiece' of a committee or group decision. . . . There is no one person who can snap his fingers and make an immediate decision. That is why lunch times in Canton last three hours."

Despite this, the Chinese get the highest possible marks from traders for coming through with everything they promise, and sometimes more. "In every case of the chemicals we bought in 1972, what arrived was better in quality than the Chinese said it would be," says Herbert G. Roskind Jr., vice president of Sobin Chemical. Veteran traders say that has always been true, enough so that some experienced buyers no longer even seek out contractual safeguards. If the Chinese can't deliver, says one, they always find a way to make amends.

China Reflections

WILL China, with one-fourth the world's population, develop into a superpower in the decades
ahead, with increased ability to challenge U.S. power
and policy?

The 19th Century saw the zenith of Britain's power
and America has been dominant on the world scene in
the 20th Century. What are the prospects that the 21st
might be China's century?

The traveler returning home after a visit to China
finds his thoughts turn increasingly from the China
of today to questions such as these about the China of
tomorrow that the U.S. will be living with in future
decades.

With the impressions of China's present primitiveness still fresh in his mind, the questions themselves
seem far-fetched. Yet the traveler cannot help reflect-
ing also on China's immense promise for the future, the
problems it must overcome if it is to realize that promise, and the potential impact on the U.S.

The present primitiveness of China's economy is
apparent as soon as you cross the border north of
Hong Kong and begin the two-hour train trip to Canton. Looking out the train window you see men strain-
ing to pedal bikes that are pulling carts loaded with
half a dozen oil drums each. Later you realize they
have it relatively easy. The roads elsewhere in the
country are full of men — and often women — har-

nessed to carts like beasts of burden and pulling huge concrete construction slabs, concrete utility poles, loads of bricks, bales of cotton and many other types of freight.

As recently as 1959 so-called native transport — porters, carts pulled by men or animals, hand-propelled sampans and sailing junks — "may have carried as much as a billion tons, or more than that carried by all forms of modern transport," according to a report on China's economy that U.S. Government experts made in May 1972 to Congress' Joint Economic Committee. In the years since 1959, increased production of trucks and railroad equipment has made native forms of transport a supplement rather than the primary means of freight movement. But the primitive methods still are in widespread use.

The Chinese have doubled their truck inventory just since 1956. But this progress has been from a narrow base. The country is estimated to have slightly over 500,000 trucks. The U.S. will produce about 2.5 million this year alone, and has a total truck inventory of nearly 20 million.

Some wag has commented that the Chinese have graduated from destitution to poverty—and there's much truth in that.

Maoism condemns aspiration to material rewards. It preaches the Spartan life, self-sacrifice and subordination of the individual's interests to the advancement of the collective society. Klaus Mehnert, in his recent book "China Returns," recalls how Khrushchev called this a beggars' communism — "a state of poverty at the subsistence level elevated into a principle, with poverty defined as virtue so as to prevent any dangerous striving for consumer goods from raising its head."

This, in many respects, is China today — a country the world regards as among the major powers, but one whose living standards and general economy are most accurately described as primitive.

But this is not necessarily the China of tomorrow. China is on the move, and we should be aware of the promise as well as the problems that could shape its future.

Its huge population—at 800 million, nearly four times that of the U.S.—can be both a strength and a weakness. But for the first time this population has been unified. Today it has a national sense of purpose, the building of a new and modern China, that is a powerful force.

The question arises: How can a people support a government or a system when it offers them such poverty compared with the living standards of the U.S., Japan, even Taiwan or South Korea?

The average Chinese is not comparing his progress with the U.S. or even Taiwan — of which he is allowed to know very little. He is not comparing a Communist system with a non-Communist alternative. He is comparing his present relative security and sense of national dignity with what preceded it—years of civil war, years of war with Japan, internal disorganization and disorder, inflation, epidemics and terrible uncertainty if not hopelessness.

One need not be an admirer of communism to perceive that the result is a national unity and motivation that must be considered one of China's great present strengths — a strength China lacked in the past.

China has other strengths that add to its promise for the future. It "has the natural resources of a superpower," in the words used by the U.S. Government expert in the report of China's economy made to the Joint Economic Committee. They added that China ranks No. 1 in hydroelectric potential, its large deposits of coal and iron ore can support a steel industry the size of America's, and oil has been found in widespread areas.

But its human resources are the most significant. The Chinese are a fairly homogeneous race with a great cultural heritage — a heritage of achievements in the arts, philosophic thought and government that goes back more than 4,000 years. Widespread gains in education and the introduction of a technological orientation indicate the talents of the Chinese people may be tapped and channeled much more effectively in the future than in the past.

Though China invented the compass, printing, gunpowder and other technology that came to the West much later, it lagged behind when the industrial revolution modernized the West and later Japan. Historian John King Fairbank of Harvard, dean of U.S. China scholars, attributes that to the essentially agrarian and bureaucratic nature of the Confucian state that prevailed in China until early in this century.

"The state monopoly over large-scale economic organizations and production was inimical to private enterprise whenever it threatened to assume large-scale proportions by the use of inventions and machinery," he has written. "Again, the abundance of manpower militated against the introduction of labor-saving mechanical devices. The dominant position of the official class and their power to tax without check by law made it difficult for new projects to develop except under their wing. The Chinese lag was in motivation rather than ability, in social circumstance rather than innate genius."

Today that lag in motivation and those particular social circumstances are gone, and China is striving to modernize.

China's industrial production has been growing an estimated 12% a year, its gross national product an estimated 8% a year. Averaging the good years and the bad, its long-term rate of GNP growth has been 4% annually over the past two decades, estimates Alexander Eckstein of the University of Michigan, an authority on China's economy. He calls this rate "quite impressive" by the long-term historical standards of present industrialized countries such as Japan.

China appears light years away from achieving the status of an economic superpower, of course. Yet it was a mere 200 years ago that the U.S. was a puny waif in the world, and the European states wielded the power. The roles were reversed in a relatively brief span of history.

Japan provides an even more striking example. It has rocketed from feudalism to industrial might in less than a century. Neither the U.S. nor Japan had economic prospects when they were starting to industrialize that were brighter than China's today.

Of course, the growth rates of Japan and the U.S. are today above China's long-term rate of 4%. One could assume the economic gap between them and China will widen rather than narrow, even as China's industrialization moves ahead.

Whether that holds true or not will depend partly on whether China can sustain the accelerated rate of expansion it has demonstrated since 1969, and partly on the future trends in the U.S., Japan and other industrial nations. If China is to realize its promise for the future, and grow at a pace exceeding 4%, it must overcome several serious problems.

One is political. China lives under an autocratic regime; it has done so throughout practically all of its history, though today's authoritarianism reaches more deeply into the ordinary citizen's life than its predecessors. One characteristic of the present regime has been recurring periods of political instability and mismanagement. That slowed China's economy in the 1958-1968 period—and could do so again.

Half the seats on the Politburo and many key ministerial posts have been vacant for more than a year because the country's major power blocs—the army, the government and party bureaucracies, the regional leaders—have been unable to agree how power and influence should be divided among them. As long as this prevails only a rash observer would predict uninterrupted peace and tranquility after Mao dies.

A second major problem springs from the contradictions between modernization and full employment. Every seven years there are as many babies born in China as the total population of the U.S. To keep food production growing as fast or faster than population, China must mechanize its agriculture. Will industry grow fast enough to absorb the millions who now harvest the cotton and rice by hand and drive the oxen who pull the plows?

The other influence on whether the gap between China's economy and ours widens or narrows—and with it, our relative power in the world—is whether our own growth accelerates, levels off or lags in future decades. And here what happens to the growth of our national spirit is every bit as important as the economic indicators.

President Nixon, in his 1972 State of the Union message, joined those who ponder to whom the future belongs by recalling how the Romans, when they lived the lean life of the military camp, overcame the Greeks when the latter grew soft. And how Rome, in turn, was overcome by the northern tribes when the Romans, too, eventually grew lax and self-indulgent.

"I think of what happened to Greece and Rome and you see what is left—only the pillars," the President said. "What has happened, of course, is that great civilizations of the past, as they have become wealthy, as they have lost their will to live, to improve, they then have become subject to the decadence that eventually destroys the civilization. The U.S. is now reaching that point. . . ."

A visit to examine China, with its problems and its promise, can end up by setting one to thinking most about America. And to wondering, will we have the self-discipline and the will, the dedication to the freedoms and other enduring values from which our own strength springs, to hold our own in the decades and centuries ahead against the disciplined sense of national purpose now driving China forward?

Appendix

Text of Premier Chou's
Talk on Lin Piao

O N October 7, 1972, Premier Chou En-lai detailed the
Chinese government's version of the downfall and
death of Lin Piao, the designated successor of Mao Tse-
tung until September 1971. This is the official transcript of Premier Chou's remarks on Lin Piao to a delegation of the American Society of Newspaper Editors
during their discussion in Peking:

Premier Chou: It was Lin Piao and his small handful who stressed on having just one successor. In his
works, Chairman Mao has always taught us to bring up
proletarian revolution. China is such a big country, how
is it possible to have only one successor?

Although Lin Piao had become the successor after
the Ninth National Congress of the Chinese Communist
Party, his mind was not at ease. He knew that he could
not really become the successor, so he engaged in conspiracy. Lin Piao relied solely on a small handful of
sworn conspirators.

The report at the Party's Ninth National Congress
was published in his name and was read out by him, but
it was not drafted by him. At first he had Chen Po-ta,
whom he trusted, to prepare a draft. But that draft was
erroneous and inconsistent with the proletarian revolutionary line, and therefore rejected by the Party Central
Committee. The political report delivered at the Party's

Ninth National Congress had been adopted by the Party Central Committee and approved by Chairman Mao. He only read it out, but his thinking ran counter to the report. He had not yet revealed his true colors then. If he had, we wouldn't have let him read the report. Yet he didn't believe that he could really succeed to the leadership, so he engaged in conspiracy and mustered a small handful of people to plot an attempt on Chairman Mao's life. But it could not have succeeded, because he had very few followers. And it was impossible for him to let more people know his plot, otherwise it would have been divulged. So this small handful of people had their hearts in their mouths all the time, for fear that their plot would become known. Last year when we criticized within the Party the erroneous thinking and political line represented by Lin Piao, he felt he could not stay on any longer.

Question: Is it that Lin Piao fled after he failed to assassinate Chairman Mao?

Premier: It is not that he failed but that he didn't dare to put his plot into practice, because it was only the scheme of a very small handful of people. It was only after Lin Piao fled that we got hold of material concerning his conspiracy. Now the entire Chinese people know about this matter. All ordinary citizens, and even children, know about it. At that time he was afraid that his designs had been exposed, so he precipitately fled abroad by plane, without having the time to make any preparations.

You may wonder, since he wanted to flee to the Soviet Union, why didn't he contact the Soviet Embassy? You should know that firstly there was no time, and secondly if he did inform the Soviet Embassy and we had got to know about it, it would have been more difficult for him to escape. From the Air Force he only managed to get such things as a chart and some call signs.

It was unknown to the overwhelming majority of the people in the Air Force, only a very few knew.

You may wonder, since he was the Deputy Supreme Commander, why couldn't he order an airplane? Indeed he had the right to order planes. But that plane was secretly ordered by his son. When we made an inquiry about it, his wife dared not admit the fact. Above him there were Chairman Mao, the Political Bureau of the Party Central Committee and the Party Central Committee. Since his wife did not admit the fact, we issued an order prohibiting all planes from taking off. That order was very effective, and throughout the country planes remained grounded. In these circumstances, as he had a guilty conscience, he thought his plot had been exposed, so he fled in great haste by the plane moved there secretly, fearing that he might be caught if he fled too late. Actually we did not at all think of arresting him, we only wished to know what he wanted that plane for. Therefore we say that while it was inevitable that his conspiracy would fail, there was an accidental element in his flight abroad and subsequent death. But once one flees abroad to defect to foreigners, whether he dies or not he will surely meet with utter ruin and shame, and that is the inevitable end of all renegades and traitors.

Question: How did the document "Notes" get leaked to the outside world?

Premier: We have distributed copies of the "Notes" to every Party branch throughout the country and let all Party members and non-Party people know about it. You can't ensure that not one out of 700 million will leak the information to the outside world. This is impossible. When issuing the copies of the "Notes" we had taken into account the possibility of leakage and considered that that wouldn't matter. But we haven't checked as to whether the "Notes" now found abroad are identical with the original "Notes."

Question: Some people said there were two planes when Lin Piao fled, and some said there was one. What was the real situation?

Premier: Only one plane left the country, and that was a British "Trident." Mongolia can testify to this. When the plane got there it failed to spot the runway of the airport and its fuel was nearly exhausted, so it had to try a forced landing. It slid over a distance on the ground, leaving behind very clear marks. When the plane landed, one of its wings first touched the ground and caught fire, and all the nine persons on board were burnt to death. The Mongolian government informed our embassy, and on the second day after the incident, our people went to the spot and were allowed to take photos and bury the bodies. The news was later carried by American and Japanese newspapers, and it only then caught the attention of the Soviet Union. It is said that they had the bodies dug out to be identified. But it was too late.

After we issued the order keeping all planes throughout the country on the ground, another plane which took off was a helicopter trying to flee abroad. Our air and anti-aircraft forces took measures and forced it to land. After the forced landing, many secret documents were discovered on board and among them we found evidence of their plot.

Question: Can the Premier be sure that Lin Piao was among the nine bodies?

Premier: Our embassy people were accompanied to the spot by officials from the Mongolian Foreign Ministry and they took photos there. Although the bodies were burnt, they were not completely destroyed and it was still possible to identify them.

Question: Was it not a critical time for China when

the order was issued for all planes to stay on the ground?

Premier: There was nothing critical. How was it critical? His plot collapsed then and there! In those days we received many foreign friends in this very room. The other day a Japanese friend said that nothing seemed to have happened here at the time.

Question: From where did the plane take off?

Premier: Don't you know that? There are many reports by foreign agencies. It was from Peitaiho. Every Chinese knows that.

Question: About this jigsaw puzzle. . . .

Premier: What puzzle? There is no puzzle about it. I have told you everything. It's much clearer than your Warren Report on the assassination of J. F. Kennedy.

Question: It's a puzzle to us.

Premier: It is no puzzle to us Chinese. All the Chinese present here know about it.

The overwhelming majority of the Chinese people will not allow such things to happen. To be a friend of China's, you must have this understanding about New China. As soon as he secretly ordered an airplane, the move was reported because it was not in accordance with our country's normal procedures. When he dared not answer to our inquiry, it showed that he was up to something. But at that time we were not sure how big the scheme was. We just ordered all airplanes to stay grounded. Thereupon people realized that something was afoot, and they all wished to observe the order. As a result, not even the navigator and the radio operator went aboard the secretly-ordered airplane, and very few people went along with him.

You must have confidence that under the leadership of Chairman Mao, the Chinese people have a great strength.